CONTENTS

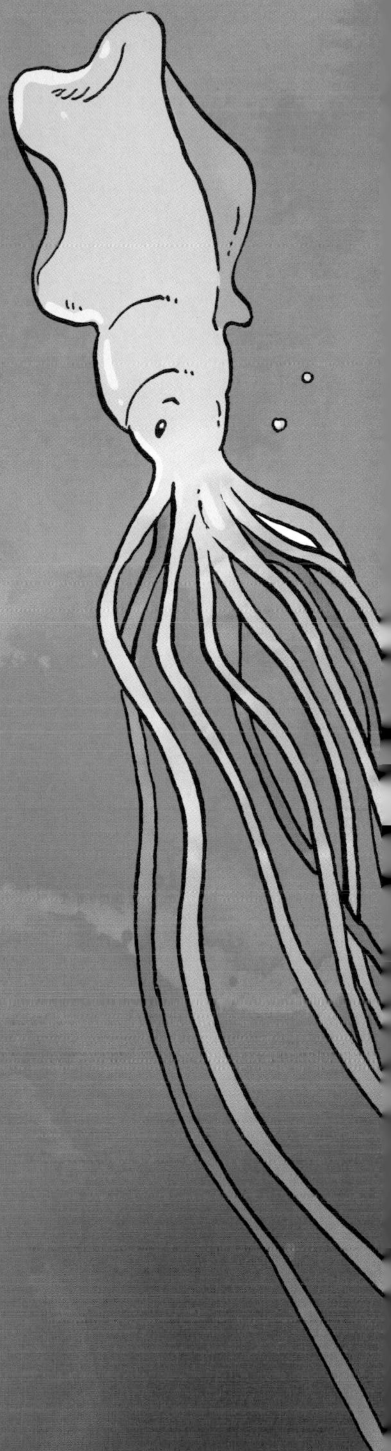

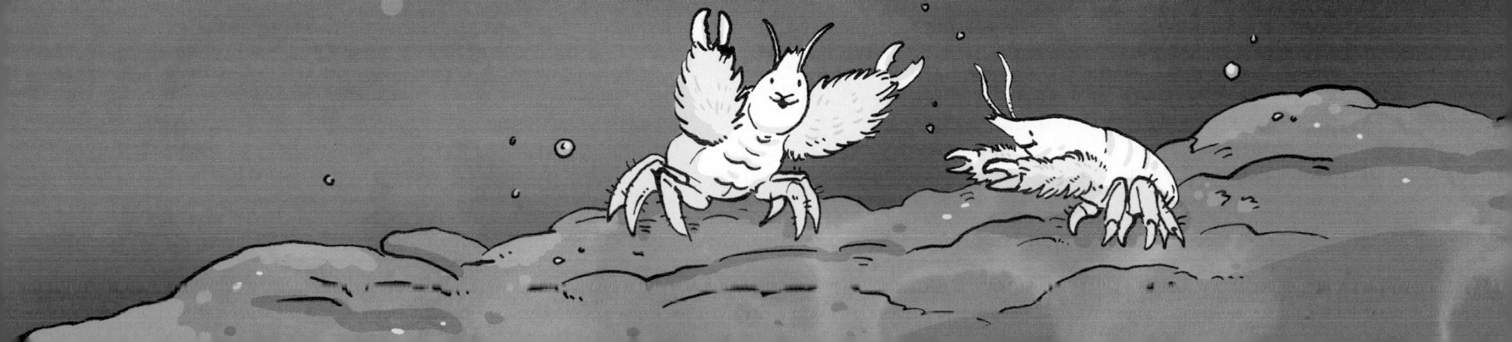

WELCOME
to the
Alien World
of
THE DEEP!

WELL, HI THERE!

Deep-Sea Hatchetfish

Gulper Eel

Telescope Fish

Ocean Layers

These are the layers of the ocean. As the ocean gets deeper, it gets colder and darker, and the pressure increases.

THE EPIPELAGIC ZONE (ep-ee-pel-AH-jik):
Known as the sunlight zone, from 0 to 650 feet

THE MESOPELAGIC ZONE (meez-oh-pel-AH-jik):
also called the twilight zone, from 650 to 3,300 feet

THE BATHYPELAGIC ZONE (ba-thuh-pel-AH-jik):
the midnight zone, from 3,000 to 13,000 feet

I LIVE IN THE MESOPELAGIC ZONE, A BIT CLOSER TO THE SURFACE!

THE ABYSSOPELAGIC ZONE (ab-iss-oh-pel-AH-jik):
Known as the abyss, from 12,124 to 19,686 feet

THE HADALPELAGIC ZONE (hade-al-pel-AH-jik):
the trenches, the deepest part of the ocean, from 19,686 to 36,100 feet

What is Pressure?

As you dive deeper in a swimming pool, there is more water above you, creating more force on top of you (so you feel pressure in your ears). Near the surface of the ocean, the pressure is less intense, but farther down, there is a huge amount of force pressed on the animals living in the deep. At the deepest point in the ocean, the pressure would feel like one hundred elephants standing on your head!

Pressure

Blob Sculpin

THE EPIPELAGIC, OR SUNLIGHT, ZONE
UP TO 650 FEET DEEP

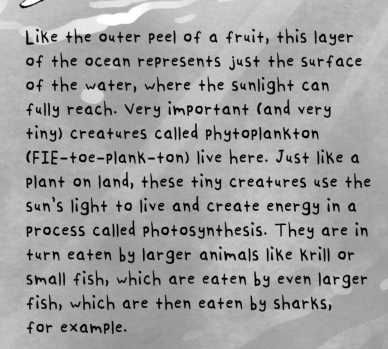

Phytoplankton

Krill

Small Fish

Large Fish

Shark

Like the outer peel of a fruit, this layer of the ocean represents just the surface of the water, where the sunlight can fully reach. Very important (and very tiny) creatures called phytoplankton (FIE-toe-plank-ton) live here. Just like a plant on land, these tiny creatures use the sun's light to live and create energy in a process called photosynthesis. They are in turn eaten by larger animals like krill or small fish, which are eaten by even larger fish, which are then eaten by sharks, for example.

The creatures in the deep rely on the food that is created in this upper layer, as food particles drift slowly to the bottom (these particles are called marine snow).

Dolphin

This layer is home to many of the most well-known creatures of the world's oceans, like great white sharks, sea turtles, stingrays, and dolphins.

Sea Turtle

Great White Shark

Stingray

WE'RE READY FOR OUR CLOSE-UP!

Viperfish

Deep-Sea Lizardfish

HEY, COME ON. THOSE GUYS HAVE HAD THEIR TIME IN THE SPOTLIGHT!

Deep-Sea Hatchetfish

THE MESOPELAGIC, OR TWILIGHT, ZONE

650–3,300 FEET DEEP

Krill

This zone is darker than the sunlight zone, but there is still the tiniest bit of light coming down from the surface. Some animals have large eyes, like the barreleye fish, to take in all the light they can.

Often, animals in the mesopelagic zone migrate up to the epipelagic zone at night to find food, like many species of squid and some fish. They rise to the surface in the evening and feed on plankton, but then when the sun comes up, they descend back to the darkness of the mesopelagic to hide from predators (animals that would like to eat them)! But some predators dive deep to follow them.

Barreleye Fish

Squid Migration

There are a QUADRILLION bristlemouth fish here in this zone. (A quadrillion is one million billion!) They are among the most numerous vertebrates (animals with a backbone) in the world.

Slender Snipe Eel

Stoplight Loosejaw Fish

Some fish here, like deep-sea hatchetfish, have large eyes and photophores (light-creating organs) on their sides, which resemble daylight and act like camouflage to hide them from predators underneath them.

Deep-Sea Hatchetfish (from below)

THE GIANT LARVACEAN

328–984 FEET DEEP

WELCOME TO MY MAGNIFICENT SNOT PALACE!

AMAZING, ISN'T IT? I MADE IT MYSELF!

Larvaceans are a type of sea squirt (also called a tunicate), which can swim freely and look a little like a three-inch tadpole.

FLOOR PLAN:

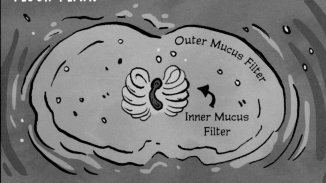

Outer Mucus Filter

Inner Mucus Filter

They create huge mucus houses that are both their home and their way to make a meal.

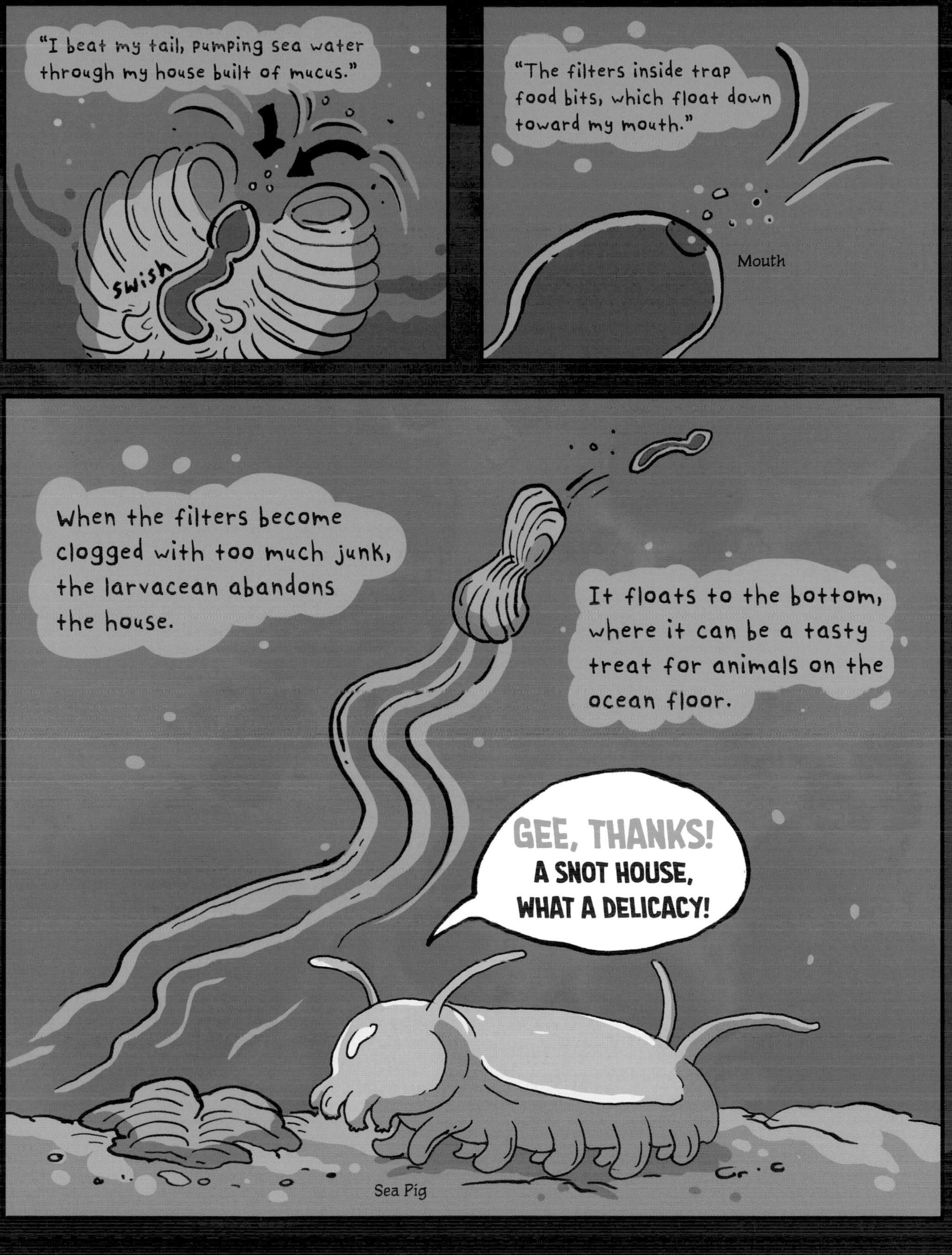

"I beat my tail, pumping sea water through my house built of mucus."
swish
"The filters inside trap food bits, which float down toward my mouth."
Mouth
When the filters become clogged with too much junk, the larvacean abandons the house.
It floats to the bottom, where it can be a tasty treat for animals on the ocean floor.
GEE, THANKS! A SNOT HOUSE, WHAT A DELICACY!
Sea Pig

SEA ANGELS

Sea angels are small swimming sea slugs, only two inches long, that look very innocent and angelic. They even fly through the water, flapping their wings.

UP TO 2,000 FEET DEEP

But when their prey (an animal that is eaten by other animals) swims by, the sea angel's horns, which are really tentacle-like arms, come out and snatch them.

Sea butterflies (a type of swimming sea snail) are the only food that a certain species of sea angels will eat (they're picky)!

BEHOLD ME, SEA BUTTERFLIES, AND QUIVER WITH FEAR!

SNAP!

They use these tentacles to remove sea butterflies from their shells and eat them up.

The sea angels start out as male but turn female throughout the course of their lives.

When they are young, sea angels have a shell, but they shed it as they grow older. Sea butterflies, on the other hand, keep their shell.

SO LONG, SHELL!

THE INCREDIBLE EYES OF THE BARRELEYE FISH

The barreleye is a deep-sea fish with a large transparent head. You can see right through it to its tubular green eyes.

(See those black dots that look like eyes? Those are actually its nares, which are like the fish's nostrils.)

THAT'S RIGHT, I CAN SEE **THROUGH MY OWN HEAD!**

These eyes swivel to look upward, like a submarine periscope, so the fish can spot prey floating above.

"There is only the tiniest bit of light coming down from above, but I can use it to see the outlines of my prey."

The barreleye has never been observed eating, but scientists believe it preys on jellies and siphonophores (a relative of jellies). Its squishy, fluid-filled head also protects it from any nasty stings.

Zap!

When it spots something to eat, the barreleye swivels its eyes to get a better look at its prey before it strikes. It then enjoys a well-earned snack.

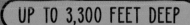

UP TO 3,300 FEET DEEP

WHO NEEDS PEANUT BUTTER? I'M ALL ABOUT THE JELLY!

SQUID of the DEEP

BIGFIN SQUID:

These squid look very haunting, like an alien about to invade Earth! They have tiny bodies but have looooooooooong arms (between thirteen and twenty-six feet) and large fins on their heads.
It is not known for sure how they feed.

LIVES IN THE
BATHYPELAGIC ZONE

PIGLET SQUID:

Also known as the reindeer squid, this adorable squid drifts along upside down. Its tentacles are above its eyes, and its siphon (a funnel-like structure that squid pump water through to move them through the water) looks like a pig's snout.

LIVES IN THE MESOPELAGIC ZONE

Baby Glass Squid ←

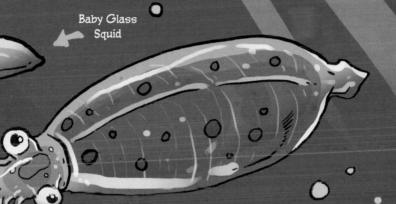

GLASS SQUID:

These beautiful squid are completely see-through. They look like glass crafted by an expert artisan. They can change their skin to a darker color to blend in with the dark waters. The baby glass squid live in shallower waters, but they descend to deeper waters as they become older.

LIVES IN THE MESOPELAGIC ZONE

THE MYSTERIOUS

The oarfish is a beautiful, dragon-like fish that can grow up to twenty-six feet long!

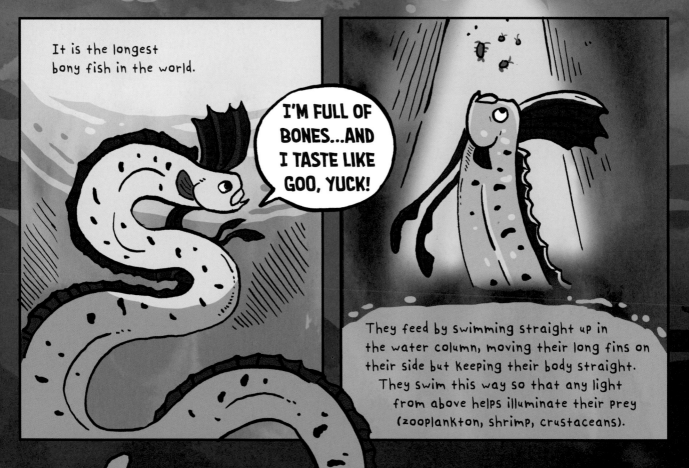

It is the longest bony fish in the world.

I'M FULL OF BONES...AND I TASTE LIKE GOO, YUCK!

They feed by swimming straight up in the water column, moving their long fins on their side but keeping their body straight. They swim this way so that any light from above helps illuminate their prey (zooplankton, shrimp, crustaceans).

OARFISH

It was believed that oarfish surfacing was an omen of an earthquake or tsunami.

OH GIVE ME A BREAK!

But scientists have found no connection between oarfish washing ashore and calamity!

Oarfish are rarely seen on the surface of the water, only coming up when they are dead or dying.

Ye Olde Oarfish!

Due to the strange looks and mysterious habits of these fish, it's no wonder people in the 1800s believed them to be sea serpents.

VELCOME! IT IS I, ZEE **VAMPIRE** SQUID!

2,000–3,000 FEET DEEP

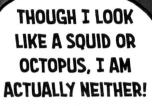

THOUGH I LOOK LIKE A SQUID OR OCTOPUS, I AM ACTUALLY NEITHER! AND I DON'T **DRINK BLOOD.**

The DREADED VAMPIRE SQUID

Vampiric Habits

To frighten predators away, the vampire squid can tuck itself inside out, into a "pineapple posture" to show off large spines!

A living fossil, it first appeared over three hundred million years ago (long before the dinosaurs)!

"There is an ancestral link between us, but I am in a group all my own."

Octopus

Vampire Squid

Squid

"What makes me unique is my curly filaments. They are long strings that I dangle out from my twelve-inch-long body to catch bits of dead animals and poo, then I retract them to eat."

"Unlike other squid and octopuses, I mainly eat nonliving food instead of living prey."

"This strategy lets me conserve energy. Vampires need their rest!"

Unlike other squid, which produce ink, the vampire squid shoots out glowing mucus from the tips of its arms, giving it enough time to confuse a predator and escape becoming its meal.

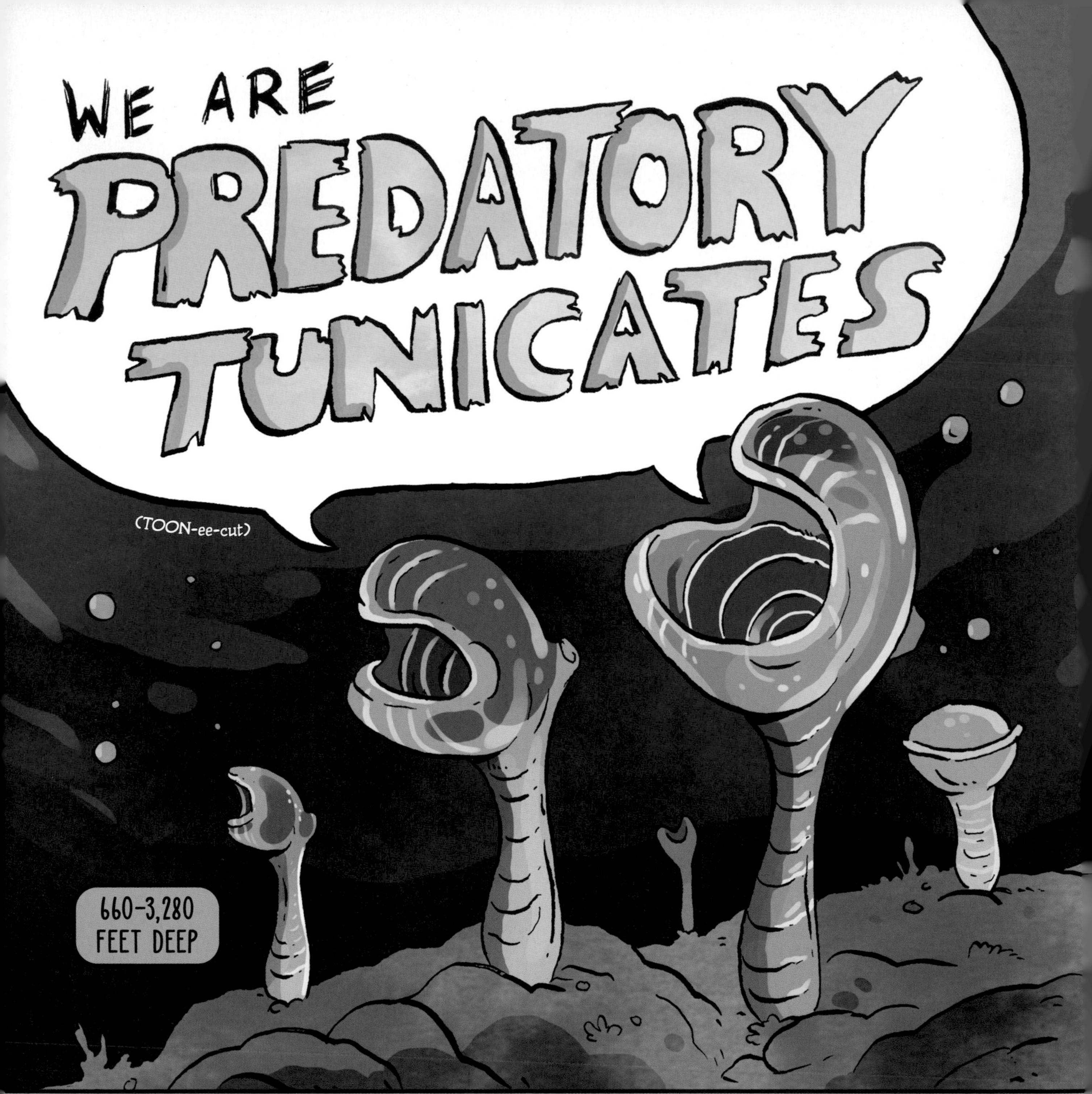
WE ARE
PREDATORY
TUNICATES
(TOON-ee-cut)
660–3,280
FEET DEEP

What Are Tunicates?

Tunicates are ocean animals that are also called sea squirts. In their free-swimming, larval form, they look similar to the giant larvacean. They have a notochord, which is a structure similar to a spine.

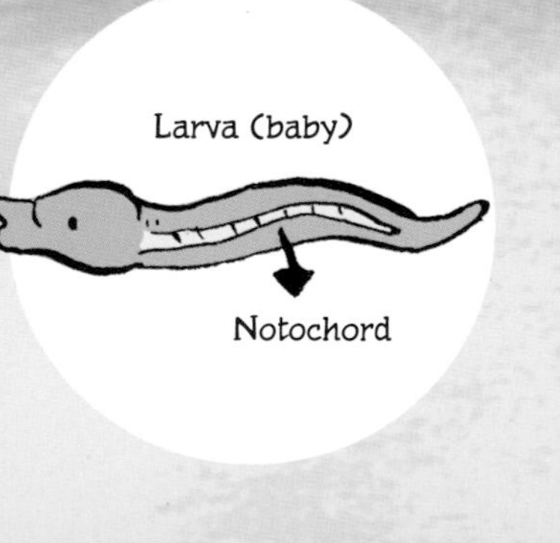
Larva (baby)
Notochord

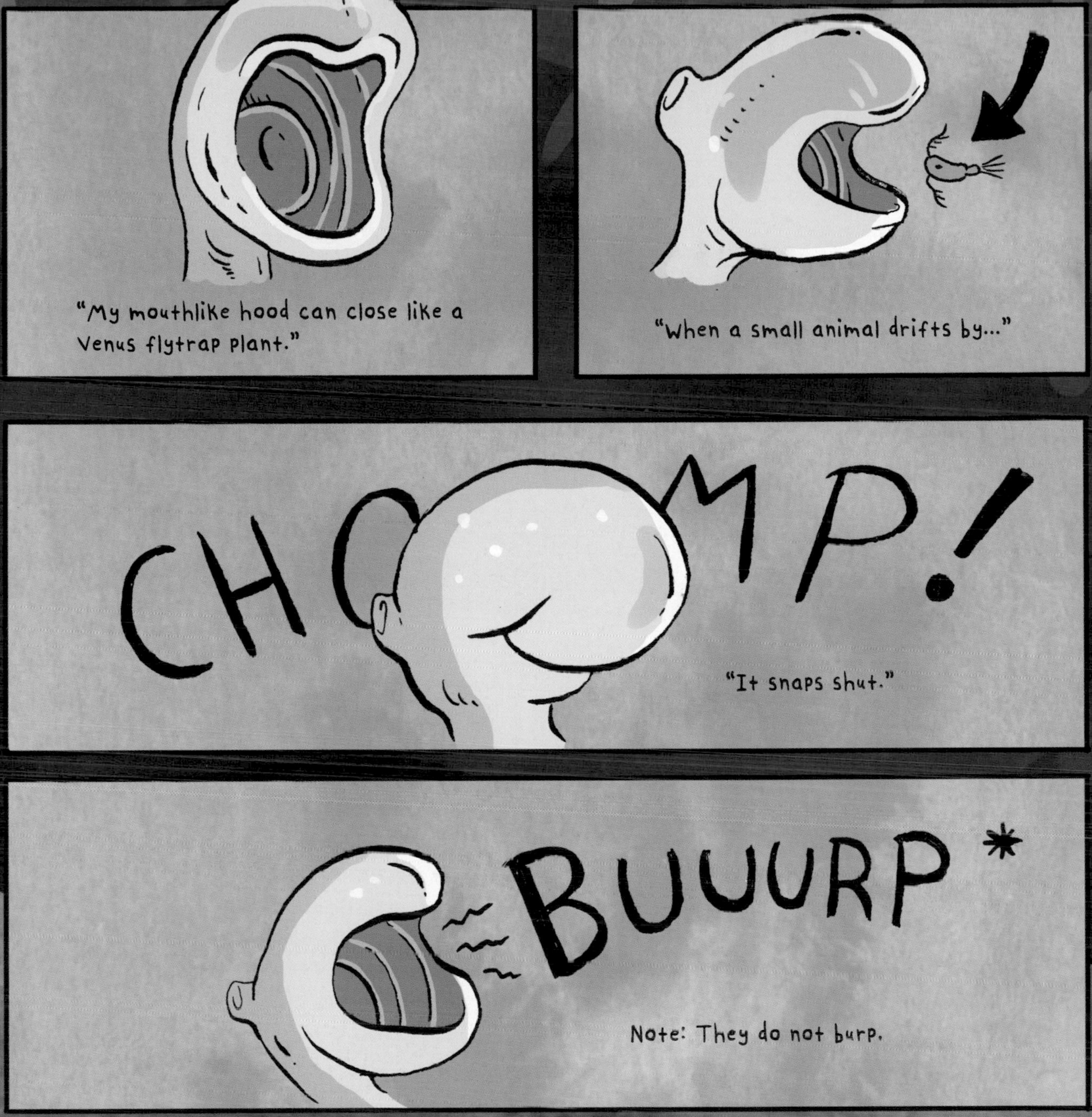
"My mouthlike hood can close like a Venus flytrap plant."
"When a small animal drifts by..."
CHOMP!
"It snaps shut."
BUUURP*
Note: They do not burp.

This means, amazingly, tunicates are distant relatives to humans!

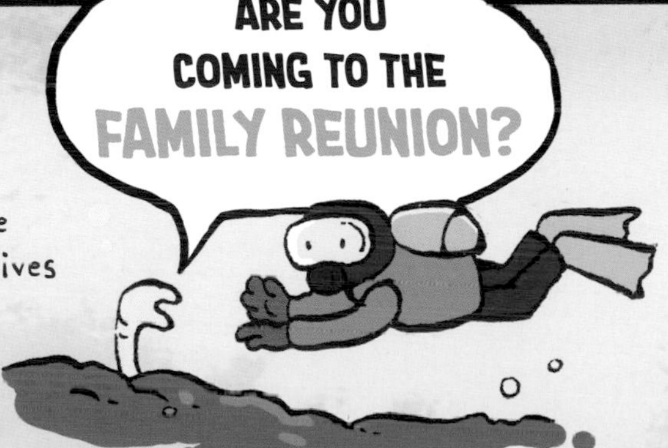
ARE YOU COMING TO THE FAMILY REUNION?

This is a typical, nonpredatory tunicate. Though it looks like a barrel-shaped tube, it is an animal! They do not have a fancy mouth that closes. They simply filter seawater for their food.

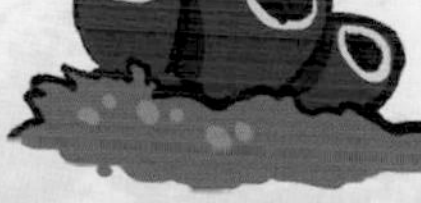

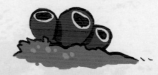

THE MIRACULOUS COELACANTH

I WAS DISCOVERED OFF THE COAST OF MADAGASCAR, STILL KICKING!

500-800 FEET DEEP

The miraculous coelacanth (SEE-low-kanth) is one of the oldest fish in the world! Everyone thought they had gone extinct, but they were wrong!

The ancient-looking coelacanth has fleshy, flexible, lobed fins, which could have once supported the fish's body on the ground.

WOW!

They are related to the first animals that decided to take the leap and leave the water to crawl up onto dry land.

"I also give birth to live young, just like a mammal, rather than laying eggs like a fish!"

The Discovery of a Lifetime!

Marjorie Courtenay-Latimer, the curator of a natural history museum in South Africa, discovered the first living modern coelacanth in 1938. She received a message from a local ship captain, letting her know of a strange fish he had found. It was later given the scientific name *Latimeria chalumnae*, after Courtenay-Latimer.

The truth is out there!

The discovery of the coelacanth made people start thinking about what other animals could be out there, hidden to the world and lost to time. Who knows what other mysterious creatures may yet be discovered in the vast waters of the ocean?

THE PRAM BUG

> **WELL, HELLO! THEY CALL ME THE PRAM BUG.**

The Pram Bug is only about an inch long, and it's a type of amphipod, which is a crustacean that looks a bit like a shrimp.

UP TO 3,280 FEET DEEP

SNIP!

"To keep my eggs safe, I create a baby carriage for them. I snip off a segment of a transparent creature called a salp and hollow out a space for my babies to live."

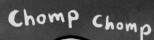

Chomp Chomp

"Unfortunately, I have to kill the salp in the process. But it's a sacrifice I'm willing to make!"

"I lay my eggs and my babies develop inside the salp, while I push it along in the sea like a baby stroller."

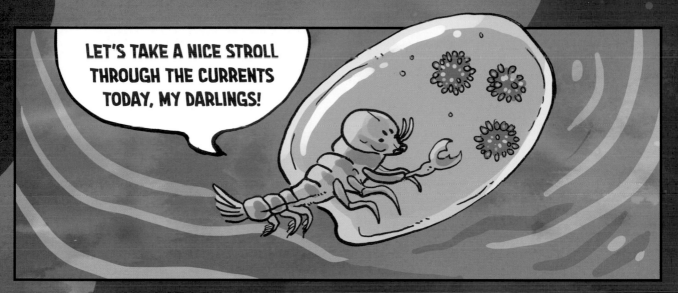

Traveling in the salp helps the pram bug conserve energy, as it doesn't have to use as much strength to keep swimming.

SIPHONOPHORES

THE DEEP-SEA HIVE MIND

WE ARE **SIPHONOPHORES** (sigh-fon-OH-fores).

NOT JUST ONE, BUT **MANY** ARE WE!

Siphonophores are a creature that is made up of many individuals (also known as a colonial organism). They are related to animals like jellies, corals, and sea anemones.

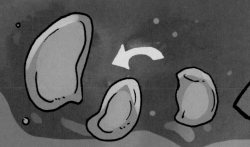

Colonial organisms clone themselves! Each individual is called a zooid, and each is assigned a certain task for the good of the colony. Some move, some feed, and some reproduce.

The tentacles of siphonophores have toxins to kill their prey. And when the prey is digested, its nutrients are then carried to the rest of the colony by the siphonophores' stem.

GIANT SIPHONOPHORE

Can grow up to 130 feet long, which is longer than a blue whale!

UP TO 3,300 FEET DEEP

HULA SKIRT SIPHONOPHORE

This siphonophore is made up of a number of bells that form a float. It can drift up toward the surface, changing the amount of gas in its float, like a hot air balloon.

2,300–3,200 FEET DEEP

MARRUS ORTHOCANNA

It extends its long tentacles as fishing lines to snag prey. The stinging cells in its tentacles are fired into the prey to paralyze and kill them.

660–2,620 FEET DEEP

THE BATHYPELAGIC, OR MIDNIGHT, ZONE

3,000–13,000 FEET DEEP

This zone is even deeper and darker than the zones above it, with increasing pressure. There is no longer any light reaching from the surface. Most of the animals here have tiny eyes or no eyes, as there is no light for them to see and therefore no use for eyes.

The color red is also not visible in the deep sea, so red creatures, like this whalefish, are less visible to predators.

EYES?
WHO NEEDS 'EM?

The midnight zone is even larger than the mesopelagic! In fact, it is the largest ecosystem (a community of animals and their environment) on Earth. But despite this, life is less plentiful in this zone.

Sperm whales can dive to this depth to hunt their favorite meal, squid, but because they are mammals, they need to return to the surface waters to breathe air.

I visited the bathypelagic zone, and all I got was this lousy T-shirt!

I'M ONLY A TOURIST HERE!

Most hydrothermal vents are located in this zone as well, where boiling, mineral-rich water spews up from huge cracks in the earth's crust, creating abundant communities of organisms that gather there.

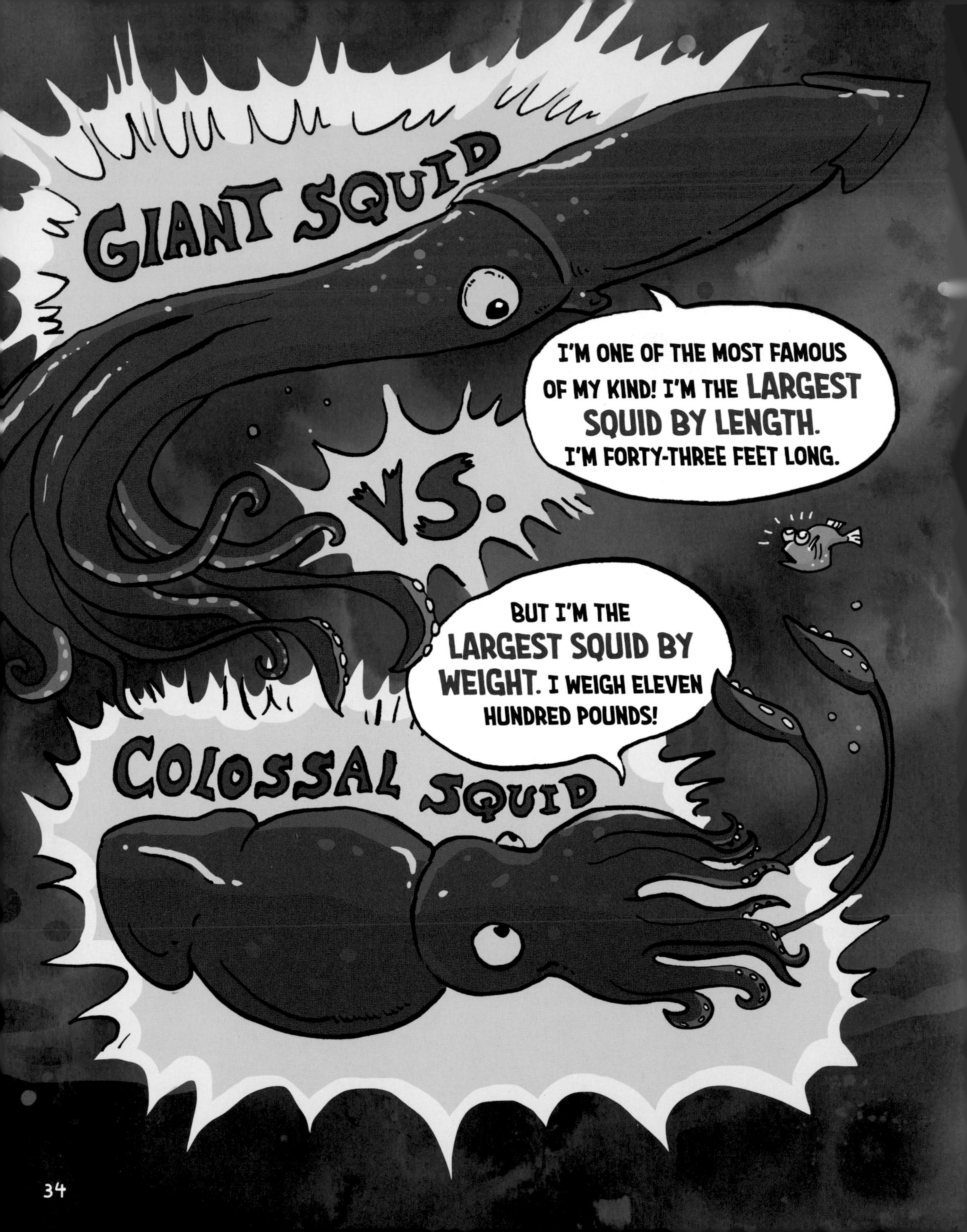
GIANT SQUID
I'M ONE OF THE MOST FAMOUS OF MY KIND! I'M THE LARGEST SQUID BY LENGTH. I'M FORTY-THREE FEET LONG.
VS.
BUT I'M THE LARGEST SQUID BY WEIGHT. I WEIGH ELEVEN HUNDRED POUNDS!
COLOSSAL SQUID

SUPERSIZE SQUID SHOWDOWN!

Both of these squid are the largest living invertebrates (animals without a backbone) in the world. Both squid have a razor-sharp beak, used to slice and eat their prey, which include shrimp, fish, and even other squid.

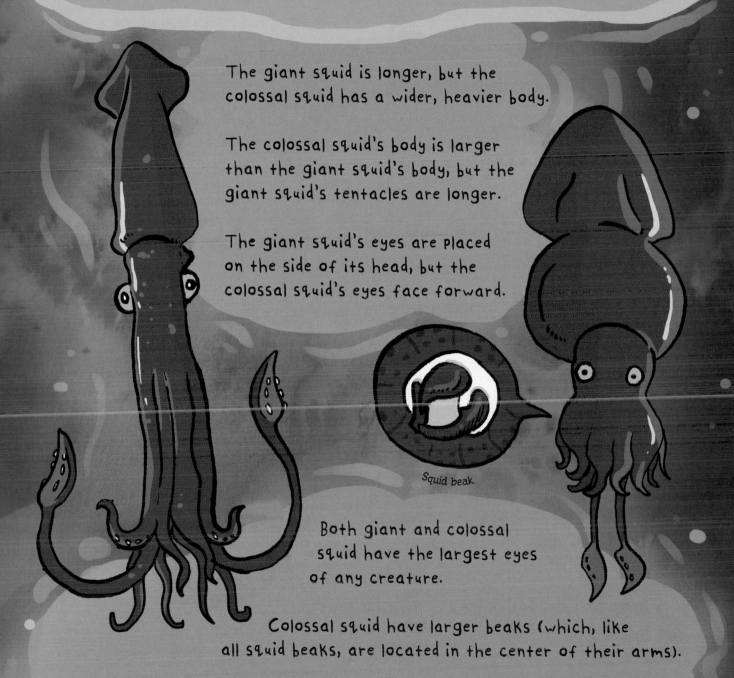

The giant squid is longer, but the colossal squid has a wider, heavier body.

The colossal squid's body is larger than the giant squid's body, but the giant squid's tentacles are longer.

The giant squid's eyes are placed on the side of its head, but the colossal squid's eyes face forward.

Squid beak

Both giant and colossal squid have the largest eyes of any creature.

Colossal squid have larger beaks (which, like all squid beaks, are located in the center of their arms).

Giant squid are found in deep ocean water across the globe, while colossal squid only live in the Southern Ocean (the ocean around Antarctica).

THE GIANT ISOPOD

I'VE BEEN TOLD I HAVE **TINY COUSINS** UP ABOVE ON DRY LAND.

Does the giant isopod look familiar to you?

That's right, they are related to your local land isopods (also known as the pill bug, wood louse, or roly-poly). But the giant isopod is more than double the size of its inch-long landlubbing relatives.

HOLY MOLY!

It can grow to up to sixteen inches long!

I-IS IT SAFE TO COME OUT NOW?

But one thing the giant isopod and the common pill bug living in your garden do have in common is that they both curl up when threatened.

Giant isopods are benthic, meaning they hang out on the seafloor. They are scavengers, feeding on anything that has drifted to the muddy bottom. A dead tuna makes a delicious meal for giant isopods and many other creatures.

How does the giant isopod navigate the deep dark sea? They have long antennae to sense and feel their way around.

They don't have many predators themselves, as they have a very hard shell and not much meat inside.

DON'T EVEN TRY IT, BUDDY. I'M SO CRUNCHY, YOU'LL BREAK A TOOTH.

550–7,020 FEET DEEP

THE GIANT OSTRACOD!

Is this an undersea UFO? No, it's a giant ostracod! (OST-rah-cod)

WHO'S HUNGRY?

An average ostracod is about the size of a tiny poppy seed...

but the GIANT ostracod is about the size of a meatball.

Ostracods are crustaceans and look a bit like a shrimp living inside a seed pod (which is why their nickname is "seed shrimp").

OUTRAGEOUS OSTRACODS

Ostracods are prehistoric! They existed 485 million years ago, long before the dinosaurs.

LISTEN UP, YOU WHIPPERSNAPPERS!

The giant ostracod has BIG eyes to catch the light and find prey, like small crustaceans called copepods, in the dark.

Copepod

YUM!

It looks a bit like an orange Ping-Pong ball.

PUT ME IN, COACH!

2,000–7,500 FEET DEEP

It swims using its flipper-like antennae like oars, spinning and tumbling through the water.

WHEEE!

What's under the shell?
Ostracods have a hinged shell (also called a carapace) to protect themselves, but underneath they resemble a shrimplike creature.

HEY, NO PEEKING. I'M NUDE UNDER HERE!

ENYPNIASTES

THEY CALL ME THE HEADLESS CHICKEN MONSTER!

BUT MY REAL NAME IS *ENYPNIASTES* (EE-nip-nee-AST-eez).

AAAAH!

1,640–16,400 FEET DEEP

"I'm a sea cucumber! I sound like I would be a part of a tasty sea salad, but I'm an invertebrate (an animal with no inside skeleton), related to sea stars and sea urchins. I'm only four to ten inches long."

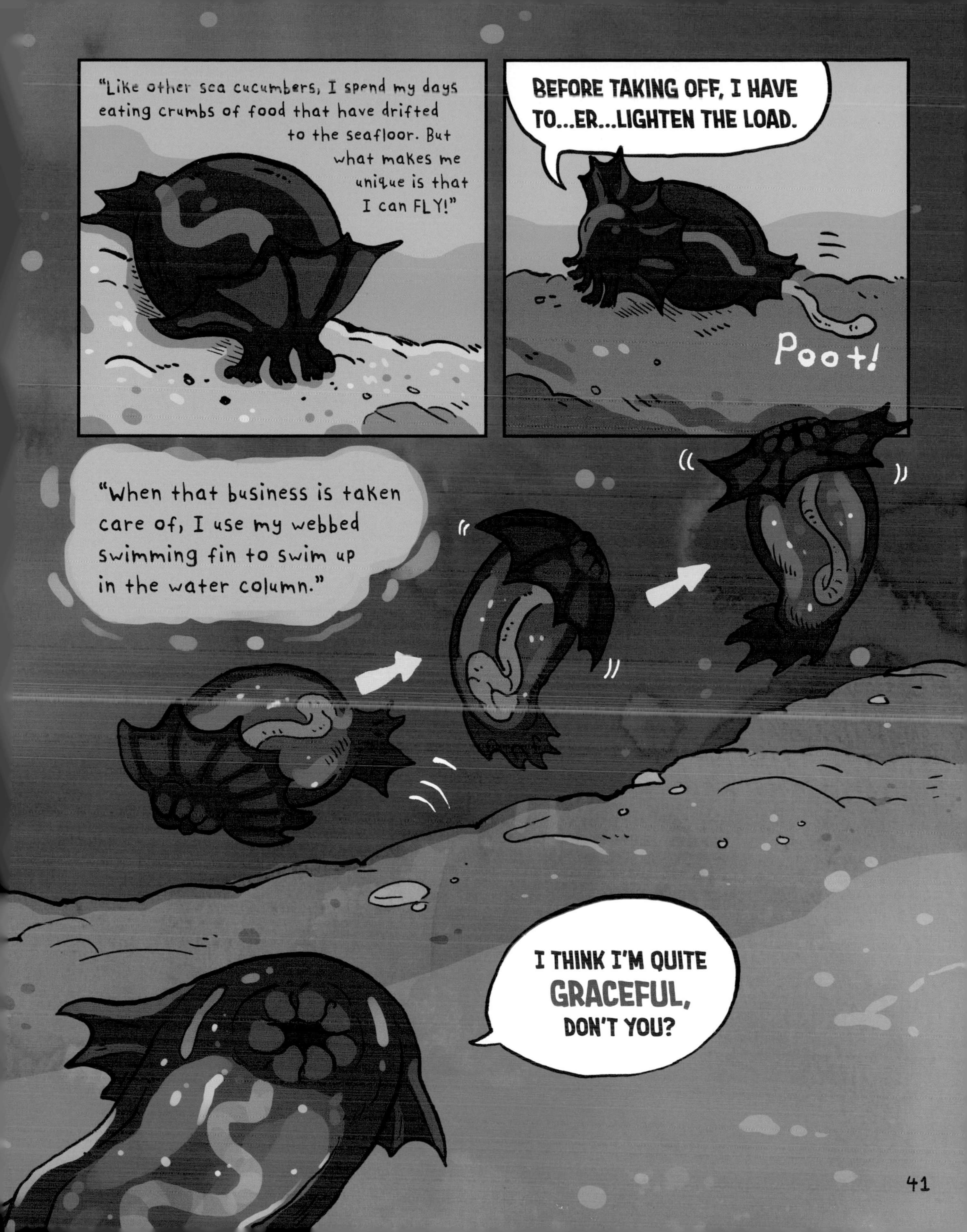
"Like other sea cucumbers, I spend my days eating crumbs of food that have drifted to the seafloor. But what makes me unique is that I can FLY!"
BEFORE TAKING OFF, I HAVE TO...ER...LIGHTEN THE LOAD.
Poot!
"When that business is taken care of, I use my webbed swimming fin to swim up in the water column."
I THINK I'M QUITE GRACEFUL, DON'T YOU?

DEEP-SEA JELLIES

Jellyfish are actually not fish at all; they are invertebrates! Scientists prefer to call them sea jellies, to make it clearer that they aren't fish.

STYGIOMEDUSA

The rare and mysterious *Stygiomedusa* (stij-ee-OH-mehd-oo-sah) jelly looks like a ghost! It has a relationship with a little fish that hides out and swims around its bell (which is its hood-shaped body).

Stygiomedusa has only four arms (up to thirty-three feet long!), which do not have stinging tentacles. Scientists believe they are used to trap prey, but one has never been observed eating.

2,460–7,175 FEET DEEP

Deepstaria

2,000–5,700 FEET DEEP

BOO!

SO...WHEN ARE YOU GOING TO START PAYING RENT?

Deepstaria is truly a strange jelly. It more resembles a plastic bag or a sheet ghost than an animal. It has no tentacles at all, and it is believed that it drifts through the sea like a living garbage bag, trapping animals inside its body.

Deepstaria often have a resident isopod, which is bright red, living in its bell. It is not well understood why, but it is believed that the isopod hitches a ride inside the jelly and eats food that gets trapped inside.

Fireworks Jelly

Little is known about this incredibly colorful species, except for the fact that it looks like exploding fireworks. Without the lights from the deep-sea exploration vessel that discovered it, its beautiful colors would have remained completely unseen in the dark.

4,000–5,000 FEET DEEP

I'M MORE BRILLIANT THAN ANY FIREWORK WHEN I'M IN THE SPOTLIGHT!

WILD WORMS
~ of the Deep Sea ~

GOSSAMER WORM

Tomopteris (tom-OPT-err-iss) is also known as a gossamer worm. Though tiny, it is a great swimmer, using its many leglike appendages, called parapodia, to move through the water, never touching the seafloor. The worm can create beautiful flashes of yellow bioluminescent mucus from their parapodia. But this is rarely seen. Scientists believe it is a method to scare away predators.

TYPICALLY FOUND IN THE
MESOPELAGIC ZONE

MAYBE I JUST
ENJOY A GOOD
LIGHT SHOW.

THE PIGBUTT WORM

2,800-4,000 FEET DEEP

It's not every day you see flying buttocks soaring through the seas! The pigbutt worm is actually a true worm, about the size of a hazelnut, but it just so happens to look exactly like a pig's rear end. Like the giant larvacean, it casts out a mucus net to catch marine snow to snack on.

Toot

THIS MIGHT LOOK LIKE A FART CLOUD, BUT IT'S REALLY MY MUCUS NET!

ZOMBIE WORMS

Osedax worms, also known as zombie worms, can ooze acid to bore into the bones of dead whales that have fallen to the seafloor. They then eat the fat that they find inside the bones. The visible worms are female. In most species, the males are microscopic, living inside the body of the one-inch-long female worm! Osedax worms are ancient and may have fed on prehistoric whales one hundred million years ago.

Female osedax worms

10,000 FEET DEEP

45

CHIMAERA

The chimaera (KAI-mare-uh) is related to sharks and rays. (They are sometimes called ghost sharks.) They look a bit stitched together, like Frankenstein's monster!

The dots on a chimaera's face and nose help them sense the electric fields of their prey in a process called electroreception.

I HAVE A **SUPERPOWERED SCHNOZ!**

8,500 FEET DEEP

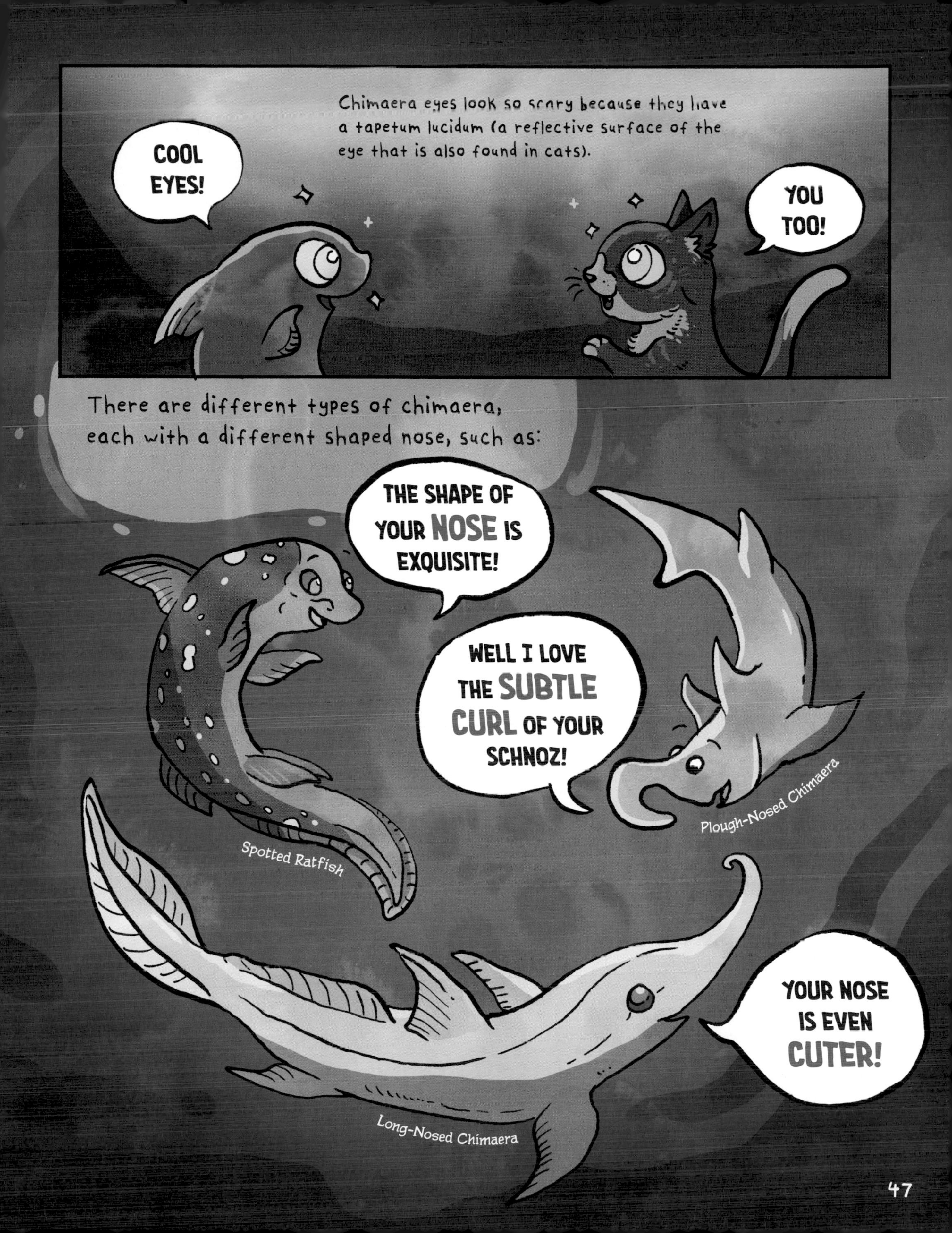
Chimaera eyes look so scary because they have a tapetum lucidum (a reflective surface of the eye that is also found in cats).
COOL EYES!
YOU TOO!
There are different types of chimaera, each with a different shaped nose, such as:
THE SHAPE OF YOUR NOSE IS EXQUISITE!
WELL I LOVE THE SUBTLE CURL OF YOUR SCHNOZ!
Spotted Ratfish
Plough-Nosed Chimaera
YOUR NOSE IS EVEN CUTER!
Long-Nosed Chimaera

ANGLERFISH

SURELY, I AM THE MOST WELL-KNOWN FISH IN THE DEEP SEA.

"I'm known for the lure at the top of my head that I bob to attract prey, like the lure on the end of a fishing pole."

"See that little growth below my fin? Yep, that's my husband. I'm about a foot long, but he's only an inch."

"He found me in the dark depths and we've been stuck together ever since! Ah...true love."

HI, HONEY!

ANYWAY, I'D LOVE YOU TO MEET SOME OF MY ANGLERFISH FAMILY!

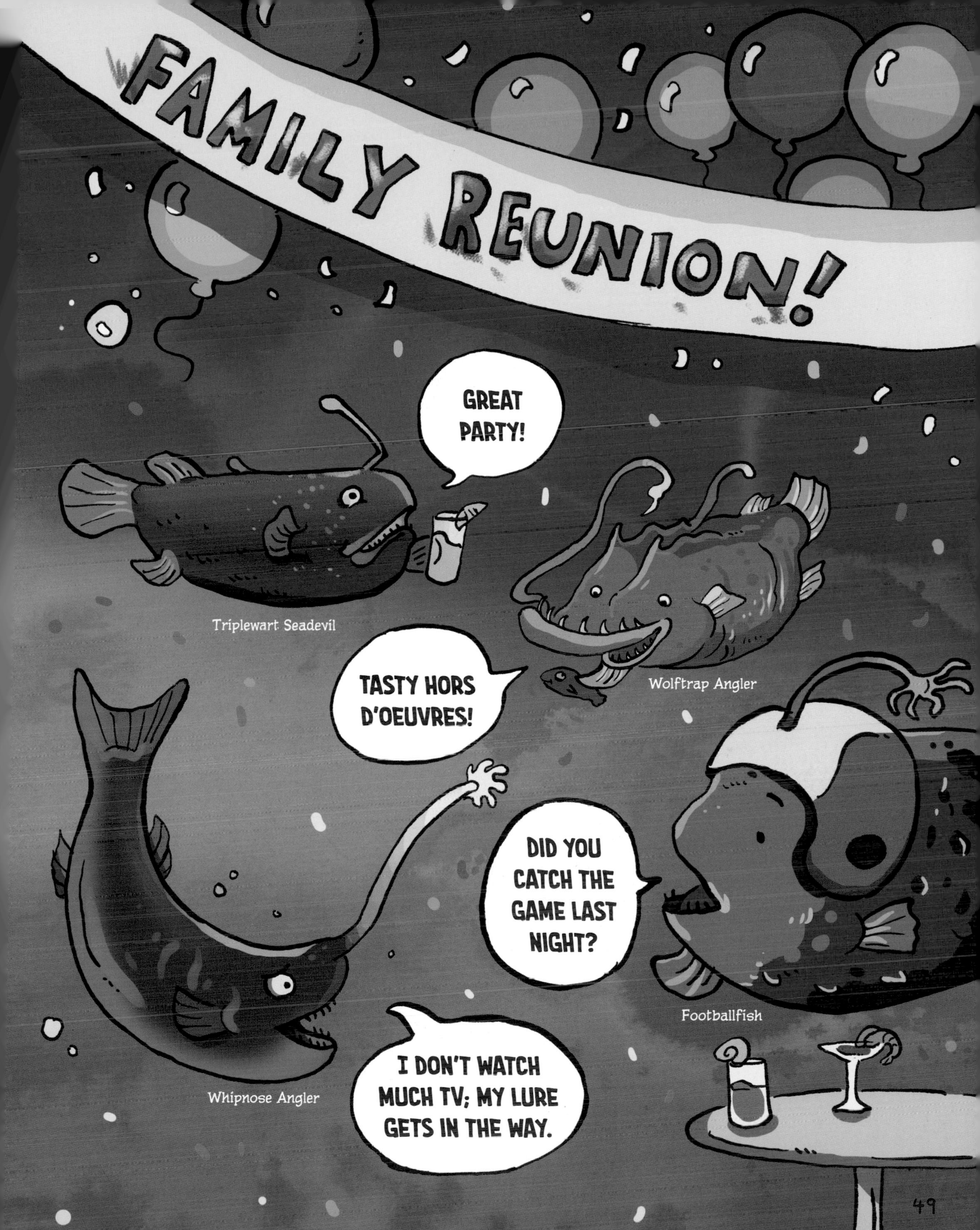
FAMILY REUNION!
GREAT PARTY!
Triplewart Seadevil
TASTY HORS D'OEUVRES!
Wolftrap Angler
DID YOU CATCH THE GAME LAST NIGHT?
Footballfish
I DON'T WATCH MUCH TV; MY LURE GETS IN THE WAY.
Whipnose Angler

GULPERS AND

THE GULPER EEL

In the deep sea, animals need to be prepared any time food comes their way. Some have developed special jaws and unusual eating abilities so they can chow down as much as they please.

"I'm a gulper eel, and my massive mouth lets me swallow prey much larger than myself."

"But if any predators try to snack on me, I can inflate myself with water to look bigger and scare them away. Boo!"

FWUMP!

Gulper eels have a glowing tip on their tail, called a photophore, which scientists believe they use to lure in prey, similar to an anglerfish.

2,297–9,006 FEET DEEP

SWALLOWERS

The Black Swallower

Hungry black swallowers can swallow prey as large as twice their own length! They digest their large meals in their see-through stomachs.

It's not wise to challenge them to a hot-dog-eating contest.

3,000–10,000 FEET DEEP

> I'M THE CHAMPION OF **COMPETITIVE EATING.**

urp...

ACK!!

Unfortunately, sometimes the fish in the black swallower's stomach starts to rot before it can be digested, and the built-up gases force the black swallower to the surface like a runaway balloon!

In fact, many unfortunate deceased black swallowers have been found on the surface this way.

HAGFISH

I HAVE MANY NAMES, NONE OF WHICH ARE VERY PLEASANT!

UP TO 5,600 FEET DEEP

Hagfish are sometimes called slime snakes and snot eels, but they are neither! They are actually jawless fish.

"My mouth, with two rows of comblike teeth (though scary to look at), helps me to chew through the tough skin of dead animals that have fallen to the seafloor."

"I produce my thick slime from the glands on my sides."

"My slime is one of the softest materials in the world (one hundred thousand times times softer than Jell-O!) and uniquely, it doesn't dry out."

Hagfish Havoc

In 2017, a truck full of hagfish crashed on an Oregon highway, spilling the slime-spewing hagfish across the road. Their slime covered the road as well as nearby cars!

SPERM WHALE

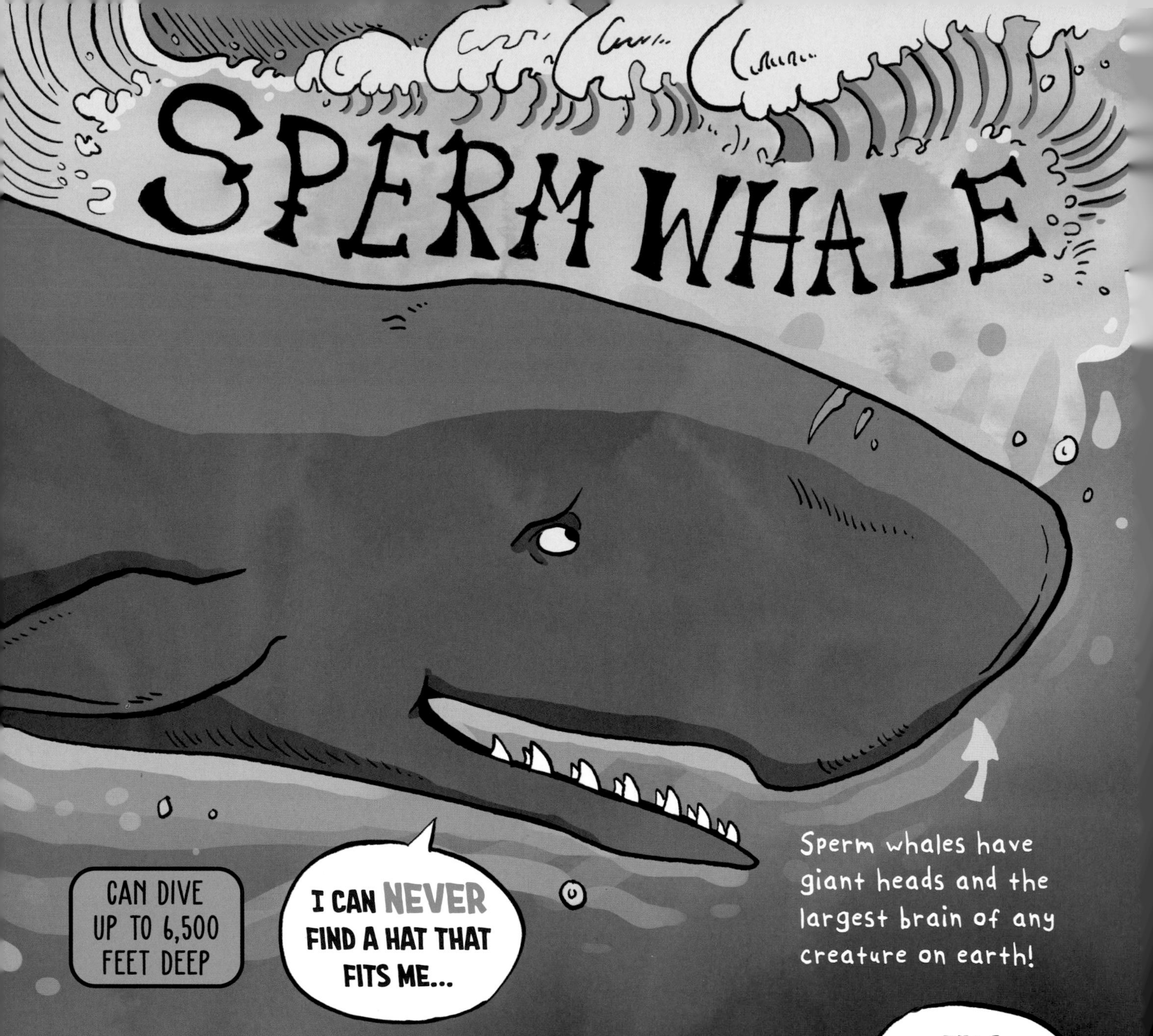
CAN DIVE UP TO 6,500 FEET DEEP
I CAN NEVER FIND A HAT THAT FITS ME...

Sperm whales have giant heads and the largest brain of any creature on earth!

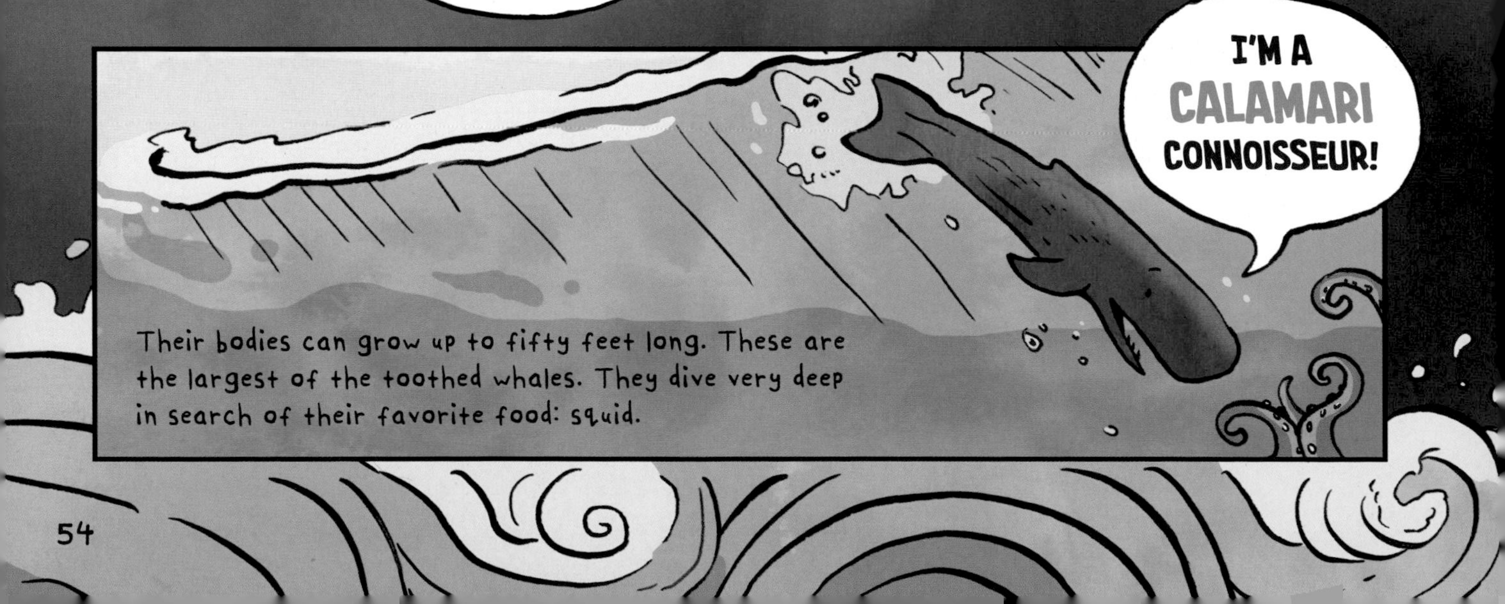
I'M A CALAMARI CONNOISSEUR!

Their bodies can grow up to fifty feet long. These are the largest of the toothed whales. They dive very deep in search of their favorite food: squid.

Spermaceti Organ

Junk
(a fatty structure)

They are named after a waxy substance called spermaceti that is found in their heads, that was prized by whalers and used in candles and oil lamps in the nineteenth and twentieth centuries.

The spermaceti is believed to help the whale create very loud clicking sounds used in echolocation--the use of sound waves to locate objects, such as prey.

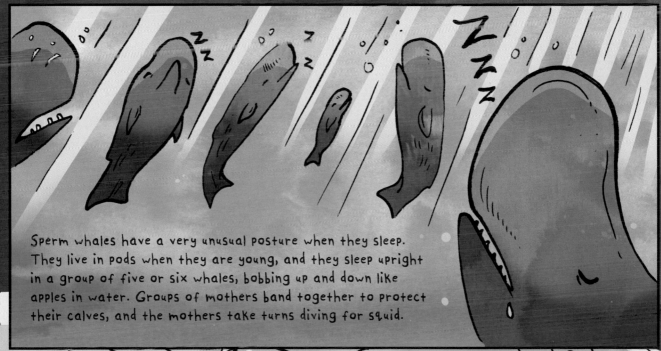

Sperm whales have a very unusual posture when they sleep. They live in pods when they are young, and they sleep upright in a group of five or six whales, bobbing up and down like apples in water. Groups of mothers band together to protect their calves, and the mothers take turns diving for squid.

THE YETI CRAB

I LOVE YOUR **HAIRY** LEGS!

I LOVE YOUR **HAIRY** ARMS!

Though mythical yetis are thought to be huge, yeti crabs are only five inches long.

7,200 FEET DEEP

Rather than the cold and snowy mountains of Nepal where the legendary yeti is said to live, the yeti crab lives near cracks on the ocean floor, called hydrothermal vents, where boiling water bubbles up. The feathery hairs on their arms are called setae (SEE-tee) and look like the hairy arms of a yeti.

By waving their arms around the hot, bacteria-rich water of the vents, the crabs capture and build up bacteria on their arm hairs.

MMM

They then nibble off the bacteria. It's their main source of food!

DELICIOUS!

MM-HMM.

MMM... HAIRY-ARM BACTERIA... A FINE DELICACY.

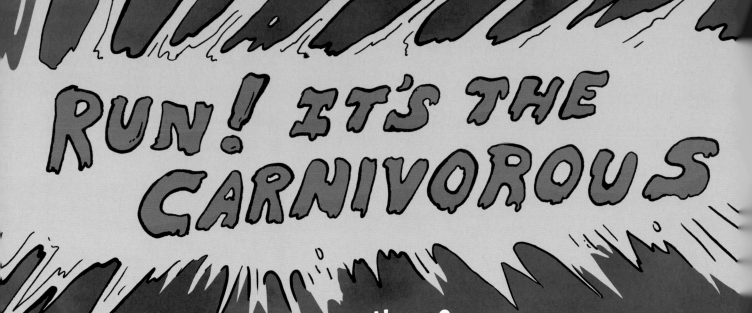

RUN! IT'S THE CARNIVOROUS

Harp Sponge

I KNOW I LOOK LIKE A HARP, BUT I'M ACTUALLY **NOT VERY MUSICAL.**

"In general, we sponges are marine animals with a body full of tiny holes that filter tiny bits of food out of the water to eat. But I'm a bit of a rebel."

10,800–11,500 FEET DEEP

"Instead of filtering water (So dull, so last season.), prey is snagged onto my hooklike spines, called spicules. Once caught, I surround my dinner in a thin membrane, then digest it...Yum!"

Spicules

SPONGES!!!

PING-PONG TREE SPONGE

I AM VERY WELL NAMED; I PRETTY MUCH LOOK LIKE A TREE... WITH PING-PONG BALLS!

"But don't let my silly appearance fool you. I am a cold-hearted predator, just like my pal the harp sponge."

8,860 FEET DEEP

"The Ping-Pong balls on my stalk are covered in spicules as well."

"A little crustacean drifting by will get their hairy limbs snagged on my spicules and from there, it's all over as I ever so slowly digest my meal..."

Sponge cells engulf the prey

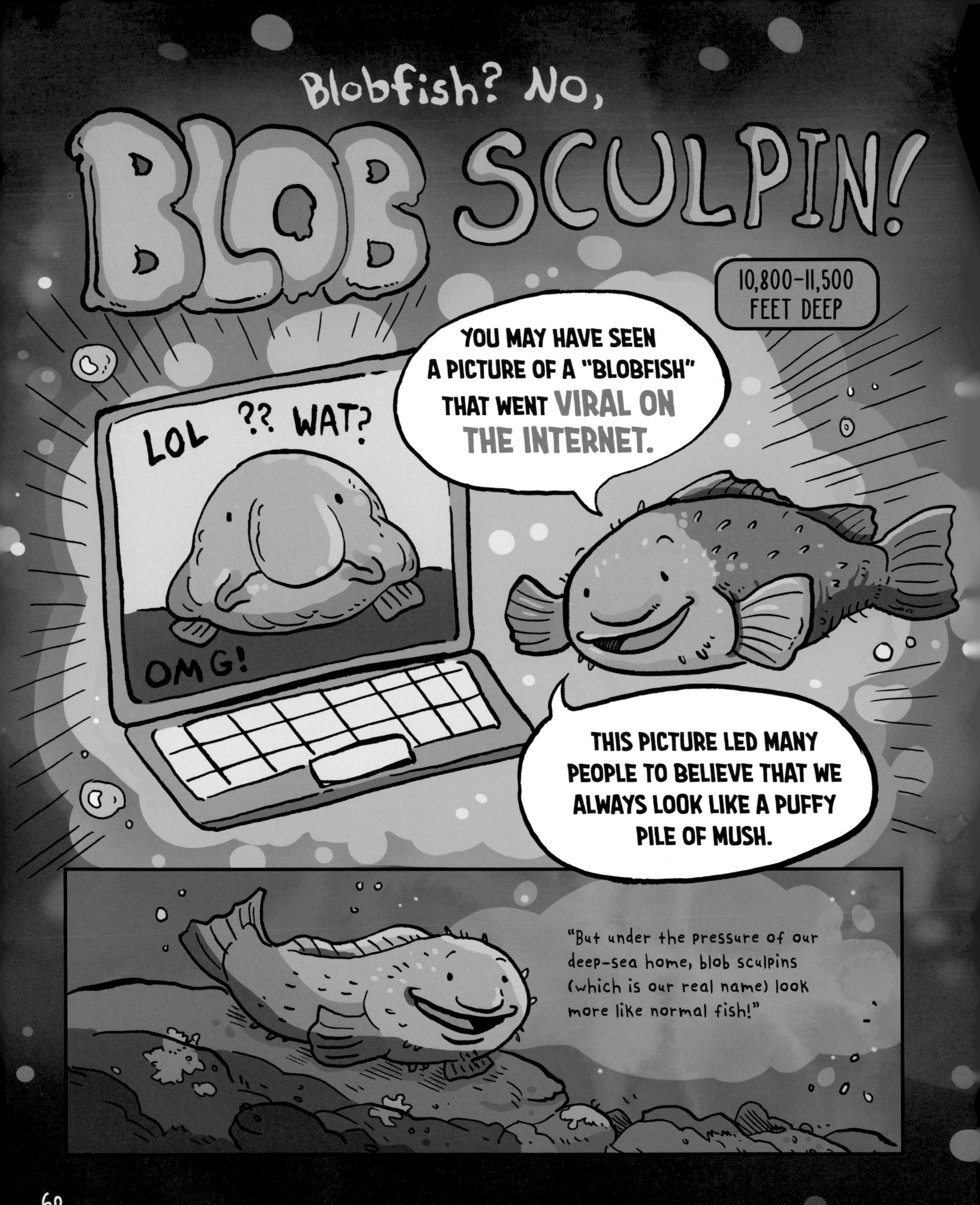
Blobfish? No,
BLOB SCULPIN!
10,800–11,500 FEET DEEP
YOU MAY HAVE SEEN A PICTURE OF A "BLOBFISH" THAT WENT VIRAL ON THE INTERNET.
LOL ?? WAT?
OMG!
THIS PICTURE LED MANY PEOPLE TO BELIEVE THAT WE ALWAYS LOOK LIKE A PUFFY PILE OF MUSH.
"But under the pressure of our deep-sea home, blob sculpins (which is our real name) look more like normal fish!"

"We, like other deep-sea fish, tend to have soft bodies, which are well suited to the high pressures of the deep."

If blob sculpin are caught by a trawling net and hoisted to the surface, the lack of pressure makes their soft body deflate and turn to mush!

"We would be much happier (and less blobby) if we were left in the sea!"

THE ABYSSOPELAGIC ZONE, OR THE ABYSS
12,124–19,686 FEET DEEP

Translated from the Greek, *abyssopelagic* means "bottomless sea." This layer is in complete darkness and is characterized by a flat plain on the ground that rises here and there in small hills.

Sea Pigs

Deep-Sea Lizardfish

This zone is HUGE (115 million square miles) and makes up 83 percent of all oceans. But just because it is large doesn't mean that it is well populated. Life is still sparse here due to the darkness, the pressure, and the extremely cold temperatures.

The waters of the abyss are very calm, as they are far below any of the stormy weather above that would create rough seas or any sort of motion.

In the shallower parts of this zone, the sediment on the seafloor is made up of microscopic zooplankton shells. In the deeper parts of the zone, the muck on the seafloor is mainly made up of brown clays (a type of soft mineral). The marine snow, flakes of dead animal matter and poop, gathers on the floor here for bottom-dwelling animals to hoover up!

Microscopic Zooplankton Shells

Sea Pens

THE DELIGHTFUL DUMBO OCTOPUS

9,800–13,000 FEET DEEP

These small octopuses flap the small flippers on their heads to flutter around the sea.

They also have a web of skin between their arms, which is why they are also called umbrella octopuses.

The Dumbo octopus is one type of umbrella octopus.

Most octopuses have an ink sac to help protect them from predators, but the Dumbo octopus doesn't.

Scientists believe that the Dumbo octopus doesn't encounter enough predators in the deep sea to have use for one.

SO JEALOUS...

What's in a Name?

Octopi, octopuses, or octopodes (ock-top-OH-deez)? What is the plural of octopus? Actually, octopuses don't mind what you decide to call them! All of these names are technically correct.

MY NAME IS SUSAN.

DEEP-SEA SHARKS

Megamouth Shark

The megamouth shark is one of the largest sharks in the world, third only to the basking shark and the whale shark. It's about sixteen feet long. Like both of them, it is also harmless to humans and feeds on plankton, the tiny--and even sometimes microscopic--organisms drifting in the sea. It is also one of the most elusive and has been observed only a few times, in the Atlantic, Pacific, and Indian Oceans.

UP TO 15,000 FEET DEEP

Frilled Shark

This shark drifts through the deep sea, looking absolutely delighted, with a big mouth filled with twenty-five rows of three hundred backward-facing teeth for holding onto prey. The shark is named for its frilly red gills.

UP TO 5,150 FEET DEEP

Goblin Shark

Shoop!

When a fish swims by, the goblin shark's upper jaw shoots out and WHOOSH! the fish is snapped up. The mouth shoots out so fast that it also creates a vacuum that helps to suction up its prey.

UP TO 4,300 FEET DEEP

Greenland Shark

Not only are they the longest-living sharks, but they also have the longest known lifespan of ALL animals with backbones.

UP TO 7,200 FEET DEEP

SLOW AND STEADY WINS THE RACE!

One of the oldest Greenland sharks ever found was determined to have been born in 1504 and was over four hundred years old!

How are they able to live so long? They have a very slow metabolism, which means that their body changes food into energy very slowly. They also grow slowly and move slowly through the water.

A certain type of crustacean, called a copepod, eats the outer layer of the Greenland shark's eye and can cause blindness, but the shark is unbothered. Since the shark relies on smell and sound, blindness in the deep dark ocean is not as harmful as it would be elsewhere. But who knows how they feel about being stuck together?

THIS IS THE SONG THAT NEVER EEENDS, IT GOES ON AND ON, MY FRIEEENDS...

TRIPOD FISH

This stilt-walking fish perches on the ocean floor on its three long fins and waits, unmoving, for plankton to drift by. It faces the water current to increase the chances of snatching a meal.

SOME MIGHT CALL ME LAZY, BUT THIS IS REALLY AN EXPERT HUNTING TACTIC...

YAWN... ZZZZZ.

"My eyes are so small, I use my sense of touch to find my prey."

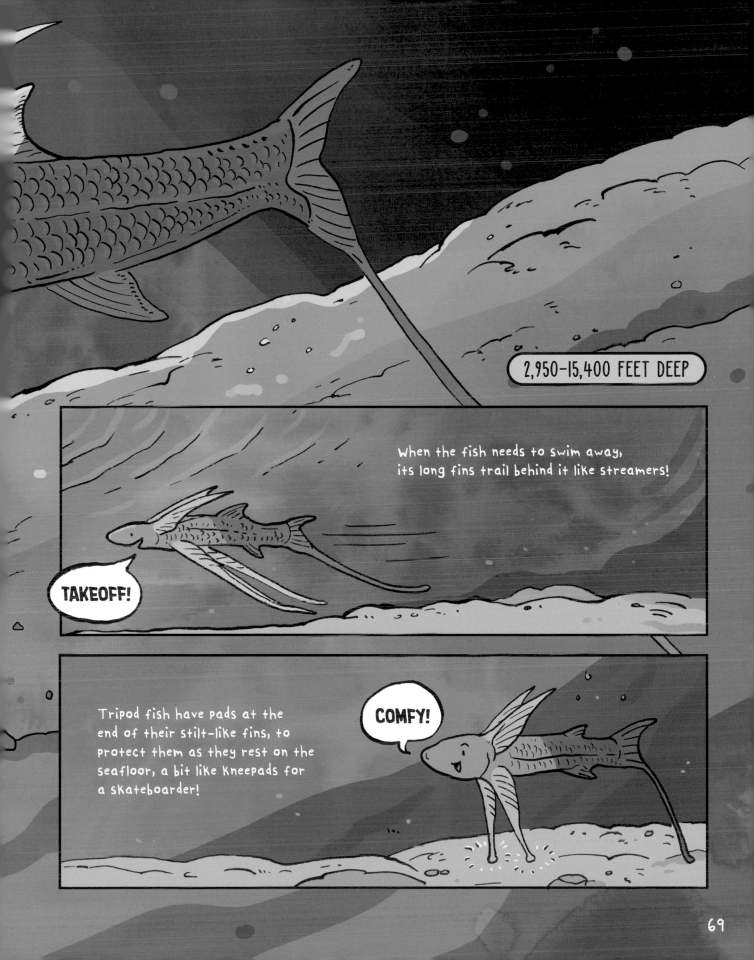

2,950–15,400 FEET DEEP

When the fish needs to swim away,
its long fins trail behind it like streamers!

TAKEOFF!

Tripod fish have pads at the
end of their stilt-like fins, to
protect them as they rest on the
seafloor, a bit like kneepads for
a skateboarder!

COMFY!

SEA PIG

Sea pigs are a type of sea cucumber. They scuttle and snuffle along the deep-sea floor, slurping up particles from the mud, much like a pig would root around the ground for food.

4,000–16,000 FEET DEEP

Sea Spider

SOME PIG

They are only four inches long, much smaller than the average pig!

Once they find a bit of food in the muddy seafloor, they use their little tentacles to pop the food into their mouth.

They have five to seven pairs of feet, and though the things on the top of their body look like antennae, they are actually another pair of feet!

Sometimes sea pigs have hitchhikers! Young king crabs have been found hitching a ride on sea pigs, possibly to avoid predators, but it's a bit of a mystery.

THE HADALPELAGIC ZONE, OR THE TRENCHES

19,686–36,100 FEET DEEP

Named after Hades, the word for the underworld in Greek mythology, the hadal zone is made up of deep-water trenches, where the abyssal plain drops off into huge chasms, or underwater ravines.

The amount of life decreases with depth, so animals are not plentiful here, but some of the notable animals here are snailfish, cusk eels, and marine crustaceans called amphipods (including the largest, *Alicella gigantea*).

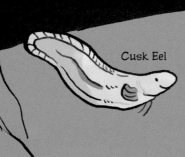
Cusk Eel

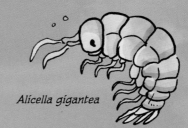
Alicella gigantea

Mariana Trench, a trench within this zone, is the deepest place on earth, located in the Pacific Ocean, near Guam. In 1960, the first expedition to the Challenger Deep, the deepest point within the trench, took place in a deep-sea submersible captained by Jacques Piccard and Don Walsh. It took five hours for them to reach the bottom!

TRIESTE

When they found life at the bottom, Piccard excitedly wrote, "Here, in an instant, was the answer that biologists had asked for decades. Could life exist in the greatest depths of the ocean? It could!"

Mariana Snailfish

CRINOIDS

Also Known as Stalked Sea Lilies

Though they appear to be flowers, sea lilies are actually animals. (They are echinoderms, like sea stars and sea urchins.)

Many crinoids are found in shallower zones, but they've been found as deep as the hadalpelagic zone.

These stalked sea lilies are rooted to the seafloor, but some sea lilies can also crawl.

I'M ONE OF THE **CREEPY-CRAWLY** CRINOIDS!

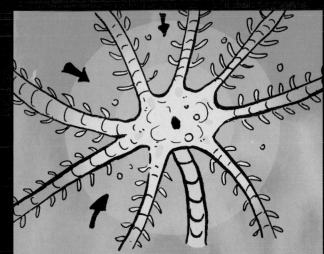

When particles of marine snow (which contains bits of dead animals and poop) drift by, they get caught in the crinoid's feather-like arms.

The particles are then slowly moved down by the crinoid's tube feet toward its mouth. They have no stomach, but food goes directly into the sea lily's intestine.

Crinoids are ancient creatures. They have been around for more than five hundred million years years. There are numerous crinoid fossils to prove it. Many crinoid fossils are small, but some rare fossils are huge. The largest one had a stem that was 130 feet long!

UP TO 19,000 FEET DEEP

MARIANA SNAILFISH

This creature lives at the deepest point in the deepest trench, the Mariana Trench. Since they don't have any predators hunting them for food, the snailfish is the main predator here, though they are only about eleven inches long.

22,000–27,000 FEET DEEP

They rule the roost, eating mainly small crustaceans.

IT MAY BE FREEZING COLD DOWN HERE, WITH UNBELIEVABLE PRESSURE, BUT WE ARE THRIVING!

How Do They Survive the Bone-Crushing Pressure?

1. They have a soft and bendy skeleton made of cartilage.

Gap!

2. They have gaps in their skull that are thought to help balance out the pressure in their bodies against the pressure of their environment.

Nature-Inspired Robots!

Inspired by the snailfish, scientists have created a soft-bodied robot that can exist in the hadal zone. Just as the snailfish has gaps between the bones in its head to decrease the pressure, the robot has spaced out electronic systems that will not break even under intense pressure. In the future, these robots could be used to monitor the health of our oceans.

DEEP-SEA ENVIRONMENTS

The Trenches

Deep underwater trenches make up the hadalpelagic zone. These trenches are formed when one tectonic plate (part of the earth's crust) is forced on top of another. The deepest trench in the world is the Mariana Trench, near the island of Guam in the Pacific Ocean.

Seamounts

Seamounts are extinct underwater volcanoes that form mountains rising thousands of feet up off the seafloor. These mountains make great homes and nurseries for young fish and deep-sea corals. Life is so plentiful on seamounts because water currents blow up the mountainside like wind, carrying nutrients up the slopes to feed plankton and other forms of life.

The Abyssal Plain

At the edge of the coast as you go deeper into the water, the coast transitions into an underwater shelf and then becomes a steep slope downward toward the deeper water. This steep slope then flattens into the abyssal plain. Abyssal plains are made up of clay and sand that blanket the ocean floor, forming smooth flat land.

Hydrothermal Vents

Hydrothermal vents are large cracks in the seafloor where superhot water blasts out in a jet, spewing up boiling, mineral-rich water. This water feeds bacteria, which in turn feed and support the plentiful communities of life surrounding the vents.

Cold Seeps

Cold seeps are similar to hydrothermal vents. But while they are still warm, they are much cooler than the hot conditions of hydrothermal vents. They also typically last longer than the vents.

THE BRINE POOL
JACUZZI of DESPAIR!

Can you imagine a lake *under* the ocean? A brine pool is a lake of extremely salty water that can exist under the sea.

Wobble TRIP!

These salty pools are very toxic to most animals if they happen to fall in. In fact, the edges of the brine pool are filled with dead creatures (like crabs, fish, and amphipods).

When an unfortunate animal enters the brine pool, they go into shock because of a lack of oxygen and severe saltiness. The brine pool becomes a graveyard and the fish and crabs that fall in essentially become pickled!

HOW DO BRINE POOLS FORM?

Long ago in the Jurassic period, there was a shallow sea where the Gulf of Mexico now exists.

That shallow sea dried up and left huge salt beds behind. The salt beds were covered by mud and sand.

Salt

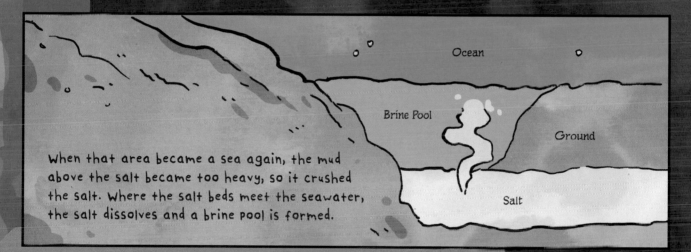

Ocean

Brine Pool

Ground

Salt

When that area became a sea again, the mud above the salt became too heavy, so it crushed the salt. Where the salt beds meet the seawater, the salt dissolves and a brine pool is formed.

Very few animals can survive in a brine pool. Mussels can survive on the edges of a pool. Hagfish can dip into the brine without being hurt, but they can't survive in it forever. The only living organisms that can survive in a brine pool are bacteria.

DEEP-SEA SURVIVAL TACTICS

Since the deep sea is not the easiest place to survive, the animals that live there have developed many different ways to make their lives easier.

MARINE SNOW IS **DELICIOUS!**

IT IS ONE OF THE MOST IMPORTANT SOURCES OF FOOD FOR MANY OF US WHO LIVE IN THE DEEP.

IT'S ACTUALLY A MIX OF DEAD ANIMAL MATTER AND PLANT MATTER.

AND DON'T FORGET **POOP!**

Crinoid

Enypniastes

Sea Pig

Pigbutt Worm

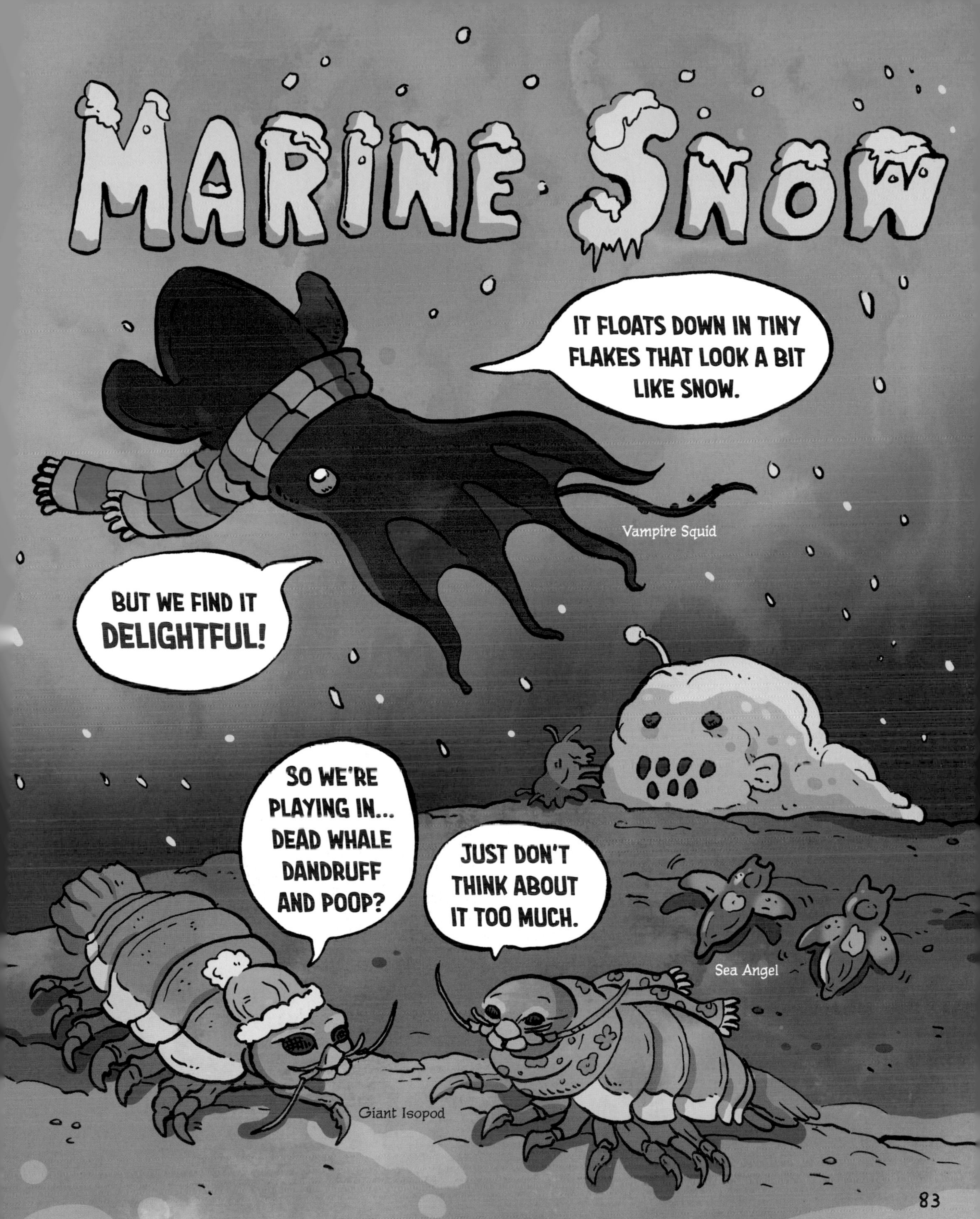
MARINE SNOW
IT FLOATS DOWN IN TINY FLAKES THAT LOOK A BIT LIKE SNOW.
Vampire Squid
BUT WE FIND IT DELIGHTFUL!
SO WE'RE PLAYING IN... DEAD WHALE DANDRUFF AND POOP?
JUST DON'T THINK ABOUT IT TOO MUCH.
Sea Angel
Giant Isopod

CHEMOSYNTHESIS

Before 1977, it was thought that all life needed the sun's light to survive. Photosynthesis is a process that uses the sun for energy...but chemosynthesis uses a different energy source: chemical-eating bacteria!

In 1977, the deep-sea submersible *Alvin* (operated by scientists at the Woods Hole Oceanographic Institute) dived deep off the Galapagos Islands, with a mission to find hydrothermal vents.

They expected to find no life at all near the boiling vents, but to everyone's surprise, they found a world of life. How could this be? And what were these animals eating?

One of the strangest animals they found were giant tube worms, which are four- to eight-foot-long worms with a bright red plume, that live inside a protective tube.

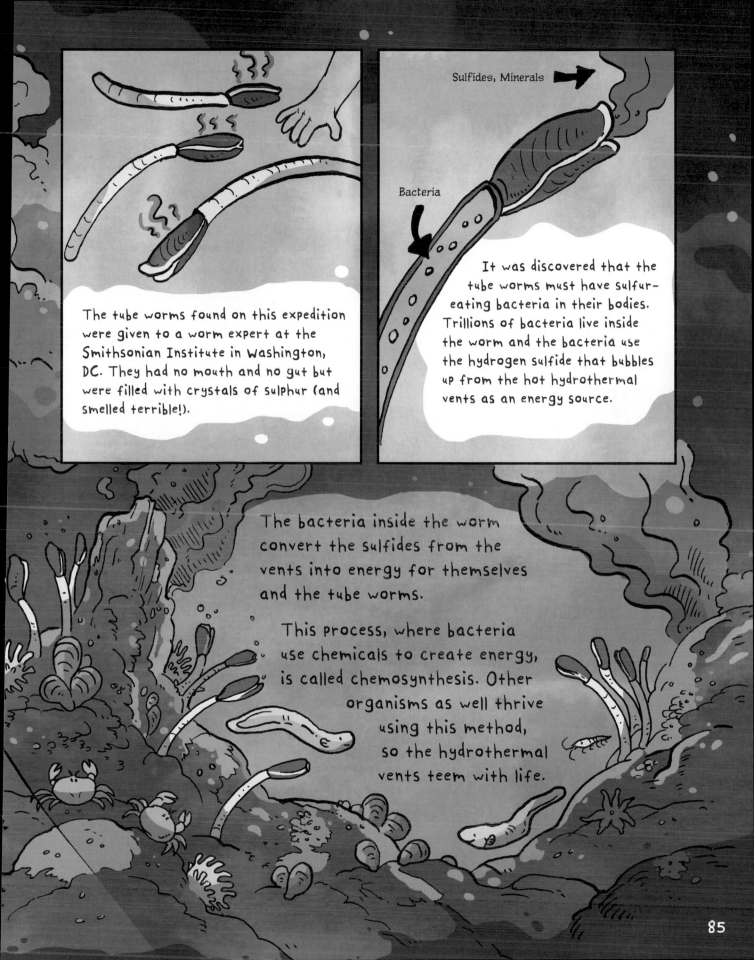

The tube worms found on this expedition were given to a worm expert at the Smithsonian Institute in Washington, DC. They had no mouth and no gut but were filled with crystals of sulphur (and smelled terrible!).

Sulfides, Minerals

Bacteria

It was discovered that the tube worms must have sulfur-eating bacteria in their bodies. Trillions of bacteria live inside the worm and the bacteria use the hydrogen sulfide that bubbles up from the hot hydrothermal vents as an energy source.

The bacteria inside the worm convert the sulfides from the vents into energy for themselves and the tube worms.

This process, where bacteria use chemicals to create energy, is called chemosynthesis. Other organisms as well thrive using this method, so the hydrothermal vents teem with life.

BIOLUMINESCENCE

Sometimes it's tough to find a friend in the inky darkness...or someone to snack on. So some creatures glow in the dark! Bioluminescence is light that is created from a chemical reaction inside a living creature.

Dragonfish

The dragonfish has a glowing photophore, an organ that produces light, on the tip of the long filament (called a barbel) on its chin, which it waggles to attract a meal.

Lantern Fish

Lantern fish are named for their tell-tale glow. Their light-producing photophores are located all over their body, from head to tail.

Uses for Bioluminescence:

Food:

The glowing spot on the belly of the cookiecutter shark makes it look like a much smaller fish. When a larger fish like a tuna swims by for a bite, the cookiecutter shark takes a bite of the tuna instead!

Attraction:

The female Bermuda fireworm creates a light show to attract mates at night.

Defense:

Sea fireflies are tiny crustaceans that release a puff of light to escape predators.

Communication:

Pyrosomes (colonial organisms made up of many individual creatures) create flashes of light to communicate with other pyrosomes.

WHALE FALL!

When whales die and sink to the ocean floor, the whale's body provides a food source for many deep-sea creatures.

Deep-Sea Octopus

Hagfish

Zombie Worms

ALL HAIL THE WHALE!

Squat Lobster

Fragile Pink Urchin

The skeleton can support life down there for many years (up to one hundred!) as a home for animals and as a source of bacteria, which thrive off of the chemical reactions created when the whale's body breaks down.

Stage 1: Mobile Scavengers

After the whale falls to the seafloor, hagfish, sleeper sharks, and amphipods consume the flesh.

Stage 2: Enrichment Opportunists

BRAINS! ...ER, I MEAN, BOOOOOONES!

Animals then move into the bones. Osedax (also known as zombie worms) were first discovered living in and eating whale bone at a whale fall.

Stage 3: Sulfophilic Stage

Bacteria break down fats in the whale bones. This creates a community of bacteria similar to the bacteria at the hydrothermal vents. These sulfur-eating bacteria live off energy released from the decay and form the basis of this undersea ecosystem, called a microbial mat.

Polychaete Worm

Microbial Mat

Bacteria

GOODBYE!

There is still SO much more to explore and discover in the hidden depths of our world's oceans. Who knows what mysterious creatures are yet to be found?

IT'S BEEN GREAT TO EAT... ER, **MEET** YOU!

TOODLE-OO!

WHAT ABOUT US?? LOOK US UP!

Brownsnout Spookfish

YEAH, GOOGLE US!

FINGERS CROSSED WE MAKE IT INTO THE **SEQUEL!**

Squidworm

COME ON DOWN AND **VISIT US** AGAIN SOON!!

LINDSEY LEIGH

has always been fascinated by learning about the world's strangest creatures. But when she learned about how life at the hydrothermal vents was only discovered as late as the 1970s, it made her want to dive into learning as much as she could about the mysteries of the deep sea. Though it is very difficult to pick a favorite creature from this book, she has a soft spot for sea pigs.

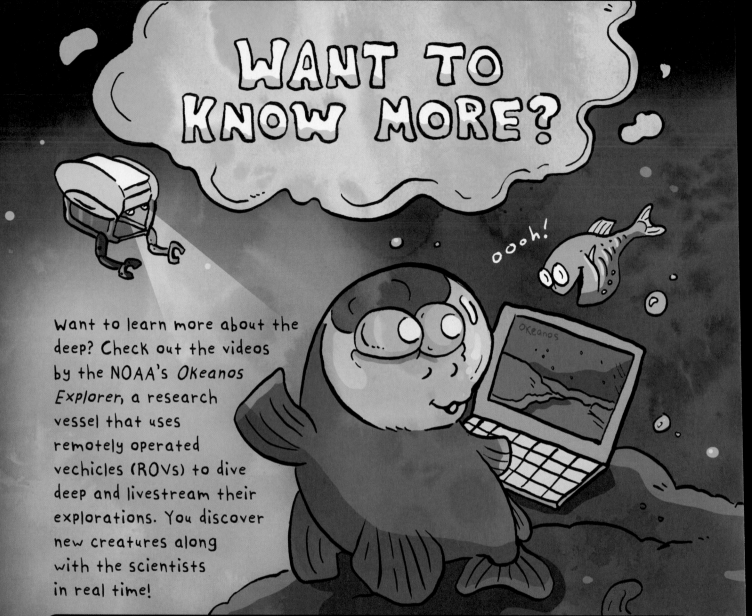

WANT TO KNOW MORE?

Want to learn more about the deep? Check out the videos by the NOAA's *Okeanos Explorer*, a research vessel that uses remotely operated vechicles (ROVs) to dive deep and livestream their explorations. You discover new creatures along with the scientists in real time!

oooh!

CHECK OUT:

- MBARI (Monterey Bay Aquarium Research Institute): www.mbari.org
- NOAA Okeanos (National Oceanic and Atmospheric Administration): oceanexplorer.noaa.gov
- Woods Hole Oceanographic Institute: www.whoi.edu
- Nautilus LIVE: nautiluslive.org

HERE'S HOW TO HELP THE DEEP SEA

Some fish we love to eat might be overfished or are caught in ways that might hurt the environment. Use websites like seafoodwatch.org to find out what types of seafood are the best to eat for the health of the ocean.

Conserve water at home. Turn off the faucet when you are brushing your teeth, and turn off the garden hose when you are done with it. Using less water helps stop wastewater from making its way into our oceans.

Plastic pollution is a big problem in our oceans, even in the deepest regions. A plastic bag was even found in the Mariana Trench, at thirty-six thousand feet deep! These plastics can be eaten by animals and harm them. The best way to help is to reduce how much plastic you and your family use.

Instead of a plastic shopping bag, ask your family if they can use--and reuse--a cloth bag for groceries. Use a reusable water bottle rather than a plastic one. Get creative about reusing items so you don't have to throw as much away!

Support the Deep-Sea Conservation Coalition to stop deep-sea mining, which scrapes the sea floor for minerals and destroys fragile ecosystems. Visit this website to find out more: www.savethehighseas.org.

Ask your family if you can volunteer at local beach or lake cleanup. The more trash you remove, the less will wash into storm drains and find its way into our oceans.

INDEX OF SEA CREATURES

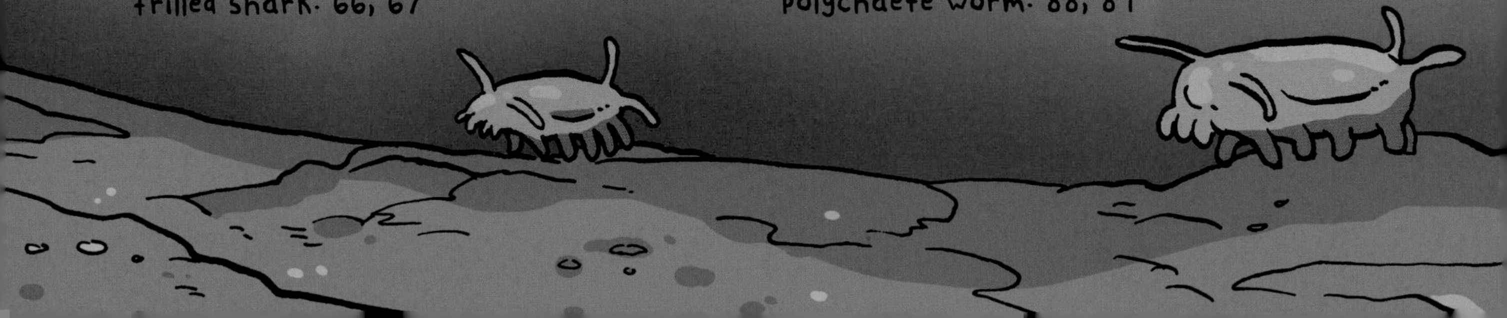

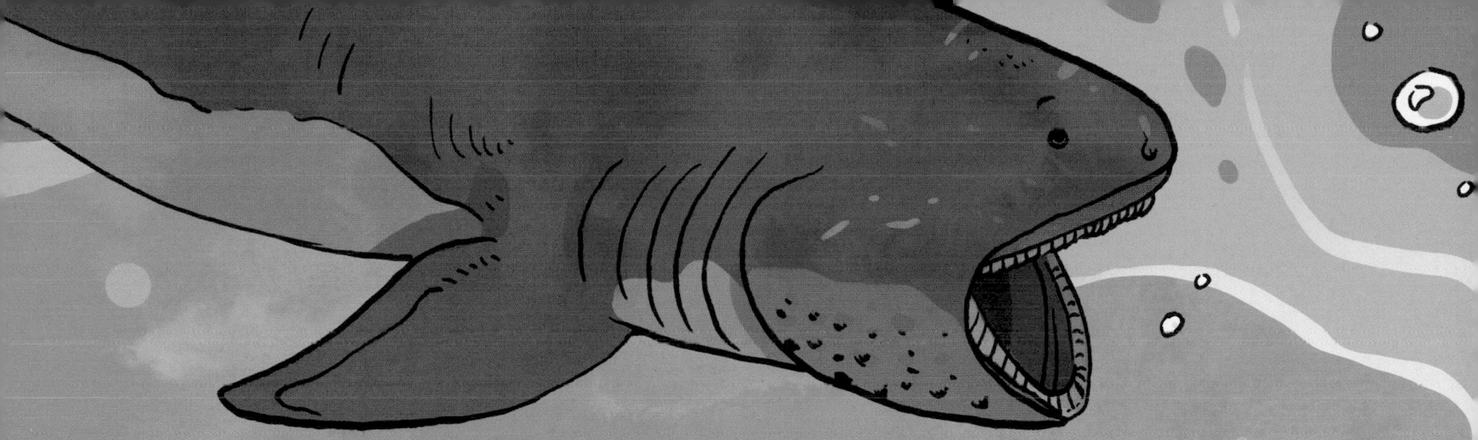

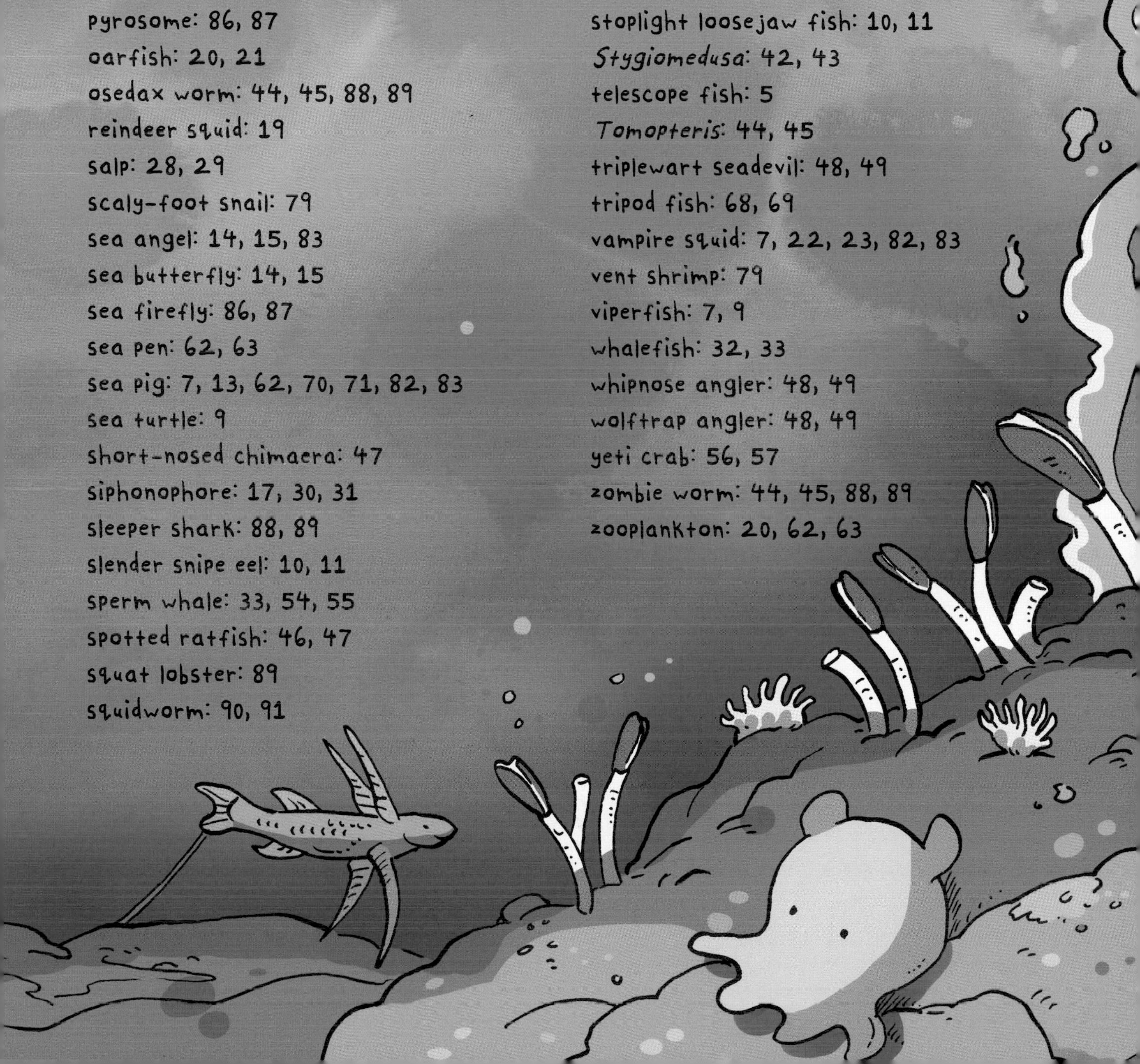